beth hillel congregation
LIBRARY
3220 big tree lane

Wilmette, Illinois 60091

presented by
Rabbi David Lincoln

Aug 1987

THE ARABS AS MASTER SLAVERS

THE ARABS AS MASTER SLAVERS

John Laffin

SBS PUBLISHING, INC.

Copyright © 1982 by John Laffin

All rights reserved. No part of this publication may be reproduced, in any form or by any means, without written permission from the Publisher.

SBS Publishing, Inc.
14 West Forest Avenue
Englewood, NJ 07631

Library of Congress Cataloging in Publication Data

Laffin, John.
   The Arabs as master slavers.

   Bibliography: p.
   1. Slavery — Arab countries.   I. Title.
HT1317.L33   1982   306'.3   81-21408
ISBN 0-89961-021-8   AACR2
ISBN 0-89961-022-6 (pbk.)

Printed in Israel by Peli Printing Works Ltd.
9 8 7 6 5 4 3 2 1

Contents

Sources and Acknowledgments	vii
Chapter I	
Slavery is Alive and Thriving	1
Chapter II	
The Rites of Slavery	10
Chapter III	
The Exploitation of East Africa	21
Chapter IV	
Saharan Slaves	32
Chapter V	
The Agony of the Sudan	41
Chapter VI	
Saudi Arabia: Slavery As Part of a Lifestyle	58
Chapter VII	
The "Official" Attitude	78
Chapter VIII	
The Slavery of Arab Women	86
Epilogue	107
Bibliography	115

Sources and Acknowledgments

I suppose my first mention must be of those slave dealers whom I saw selling African slaves at a market in Jibouti in April 1956, since they were the initial "inspiration" for this book. I was to see other aspects of the slave trade, but the Jibouti incident was such a degrading and distressing experience that it remained vivid in the memory.

To write with any authority about slavery, past or present, is virtually impossible without the informed assistance of the Anti-Slavery Society. I acknowledge with gratitude the help of the Society's secretary, Colonel J. R. P. Montgomery, M. C., and his permission to quote from the Society's journal, *The Anti-Slavery Reporter*, long regarded as the most reliable source of information on slavery in all its forms. Mrs. M. Alexander-Sinclair of the Society's staff was also most helpful, as were the librarian and staff of Rhodes House Library, Oxford, the repository of accumulated letters and documents of the Anti-Slavery Society. During travels in African and Arab lands I talked slavery with many scholars and historians and with some diplomats; in particular I must thank Dr. Ibrahim Awad of Kuwait for allowing me access to his unique collection of documents on Arab slavers. Finally, once again, I thank my wife for her patient assistance in the accumulation of information and its preparation for this book.

J.L.

THE ARABS AS MASTER SLAVERS

I
Slavery is Alive and Thriving

Slavery is no more dead than are poverty and hunger. Yet in most of the western world is a belief that the nearest thing to slavery is the slave labor of the Soviet Union and that this, however infamous, is a political aberration rather than slavery in the historical sense. Many people believe that real slavery was radically reduced by Lord Wilberforce's great reforms of the early nineteenth century and practically eliminated by the American Civil War.

This is a naive notion. Traditional slavery — trading in human beings and ownership of one person by another — has never ceased.

Modern studies of slavery compel attention to the trans-Atlantic slave trade, with a rather dim focus on the Indian Ocean and the east coast of Africa. Yet, centuries before the first slave crossed the Atlantic, slaves were of critical importance in another part of tropical Africa's export trade — the overland route across the Sahara. And slave caravans were still snaking across the great desert many decades after the last slave sailed westwards to the New World. In location, too, all eyes have been fixed by some curious compulsion on the west coasts of tropical Africa, to the neglect of the vast interior where Moslem states and social groups provided a thriving domestic market to supplement the trans-Saharan export business. Similarly, slavery on Africa's east coast was amply documented by explorers, missionaries and ships' captains until the end of the nineteenth century, but it has had relatively little mention since then.

While slavery cannot be described as rife in the latter part of the twentieth century, slavery persists as an institution and as a practice, notably in the Arab world. Its influence is so profound on Arab and Moslem attitudes that it can be shown to extend from the fundamental relationship of dealer, owner and slave to a much more complex situation involving world economics. Man's degradation of man by slavery is radically influencing the human and political relations of a large part of the world in our time.

Slavery between Africa and the Americas — one the source, the other the market — has always obscured, for the western world, the vision of slavery in other regions. One reason for this is that the American slave trade was pioneered, developed and exploited by people speaking the major European languages; negotiations took place in English and French, easy to read about and talk about. And, geographically, it was more visible; slaves were advertised and put up for sale quite openly in the American and West Indian markets and they were seen by countless travelers.

What the European and American public did not realize was that few Europeans had been involved in rounding up the Negroes in the first place. They were the middle men who bought the slaves on the African coast — by contract and at auction — and shipped them to the Americas.

The slave trade was first begun in Africa by the Arabs; they were the procurers and the suppliers. Soon after the Arabs began to conquer North Africa, the first written record was made of their desire for African slaves; an agreement was signed with Nubia after the conquest of Egypt in the year 641, which stated that the Nubians should pay yearly "360 slaves to the leader of the Moslems of the middle class of slaves in your country, with healthy bodies, males and females. . . ."

From the earliest period of the history of Islam in Africa, slaves were frequently mentioned as tribute or taxes paid to political superiors. Some Arab conquerors imposed on various rulers an annual tribute of slaves, perhaps as many as 1,000. And as a permanent reminder of the vassal's obligations these invading chiefs would cut off an ear or finger.

The Arabs had many centuries of experience in slave trading before the European entrepreneurs saw money in the business, and they knew every trick of the trade — how to ambush Negroes, how to deceive them, where to find their hiding-places. Some even kept registers so they would not waste time in too frequently visiting a certain area; time was necessary for a tribe to build itself up before the next crop of slaves was ready. If any race deserves the title of "the great slavers," it is the Arabs — and so deeply has the master-slave philosophy permeated Arab attitudes that it affects modern Arab external relationships.

Wilberforce's reforms cannot be too highly praised, but even in forcing a change of historical direction he merely *began* the movement towards the end of slavery. He induced the British government to act in 1807 but had a lot of trouble with the French until he obtained from the Congress of Vienna the prohibition of the slave trade on coasts of West Africa. Always the gap between enactment of such laws and their enforcement was vast and slow to bridge. Between 1811 and 1820, 116,000 Africans were taken to Cuba. In 1822 alone no fewer than 60,000 were sold in Brazil. It took the anti-slavers 27 years' agitation to convert Portugal to humanitarianism, 45 years the United States and 72 years Brazil. They never did eradicate slavery in Arabia.

Even after the British reforms, English and American entrepreneurs continued to engage in profitable slavery, though not always from the traditional collecting grounds of West Africa. "Blackbirding" became a successful enterprise in the South Pacific, where ships' captains provided Kanakas for the Queensland sugar plantations. The Dutch were engaged in finding slaves for their settlements in the East Indies; the Portuguese rounded up others for their plantations in Angola and Mozambique; and the Spaniards for parts of central America.

Most European races have engaged in slavery and have been guilty of brutal practices. But in mitigation it says much for the western way of life that from the beginning strong social forces opposed slavery and fought to stamp it out. Except by those who directly profited from it, no attempt was made to hide its existence; the reformers shouted the truth in parliaments and newspapers. And in the end it was public opinion and social conscience — as much as legislation — which ended in Christendom one of the most pernicious of human evils.

Those who were given the duty of stopping slavery were sometimes direct and forceful in method. British Royal Navy captains on anti-slavery patrol not infrequently hoisted slavers to the yardarm — by the neck. Boats crews ordered away to board slave ships often saved their captains the trouble of hanging the slavers; they laid about them with their cutlasses and kicked the slavers' corpses overboard.

During the latter part of the nineteenth century British gunboats and military expeditions penetrated deep into African and south-east Asian jungles to punish kings and princes for engaging in slavery. If their measures sometimes appear stern they also reflect the depth of the feeling of collective guilt among the British throughout the nineteenth century and the earlier part of the twentieth.

The Arabs kept right on slaving. As a modern student of slavery has observed, "The Arabs provided an ever-hungry market for slaves, they promoted and supported wars between chiefs, and by the power of their guns, they controlled huge areas."[1]

Wealthy Arabs, in a score of countries and hundreds of social groups, indulged themselves in luxury-slaves whose duties were no more than frivolous. Half a dozen would stand by to help their master mount a horse and then would trot after him carrying his weapons and accoutrements.

[1] Leda Farrant, *Tippu Tip and the East African Slave Trade*.

Other masters retained scores of female slaves to fan them, massage them or "amuse" them. A rich master hardly lifted his hand; he sat motionless while slaves placed food in his mouth at mealtimes.

But several nations actively fought slavery, and in 1919 the League of Nations outlawed it. Later the Universal Declaration of Human Rights, voted by the United Nations General Assembly on December 10, 1948 — though not ratified by every state — prohibited slavery: "No one shall be held in slavery or servitude. Slavery and the slave trade are prohibited in all forms."

Yet in 1956 in Jibouti [now Somalia], I saw a slave auction outside a large warehouse near the docks. It served, I was told at the time, as a transit auction rather than a final sale. Africans from around Lake Chad, then part of French West Africa, had been brought across the continent en route to Arabia. The Arab slavers, some of whom were said locally to be directed by a Frenchman, did not themselves take their captives across the Red Sea to the markets of Jedda and Medina; rather, having convoyed the slaves to Jibouti, they sold them to dealers from Arabia who then escorted them across the sea for the real sale.

Men, women and children were brought from the warehouse and paraded on a raised platform so that all dealers could clearly see them. A trader would nudge a slave's jaw with a stick and the man would open his mouth to display his teeth. Another probe with the stick and he would flex his arm muscles. Young women were forced to expose their breasts and buttocks. A dispute developed over the virginity of a tall young ebony woman, and during the hour-long argument she was forced to squat while one of the most prominent buyers examined her with his fingers. She was terrified; her trembling was visible fifty yards away.

Occasionally children were sold in batches. They did not cry, mainly, I think, because they had no tears left, but they held tightly to one another and kept looking around as if for help. Boys of about ten or twelve had their anuses examined; homosexual buyers are fussy about disease.

The haggling was brisk even by Oriental standards; perhaps 200 slaves changed hands while I was present. I saw only one man in chains, presumably because he was violent. Many observers have described whole cargoes of slaves in chains, but at Jibouti bonds were hardly necessary since a runaway slave had nowhere to hide. In the desert, too, chains are unnecessary; a slave convoy is kept together by the need for water and only the slavers know where to find waterholes.

Anybody who has witnessed a slave sale can never forget it; the scene is embarrassing and haunting because of the indignity and humiliation. I remember shaking my head in disbelief, trying to pretend I was watching some kind of objectionable but not really evil entertainment, like a sex act in a Beirut night club. But at least in the nightclub the performers were volunteers, depraved though they might be. These Africans were in a foreign market by force; dragged away from their homes, they could not fully understand what was happening because they spoke no Arabic. I also remember wishing that a party of Royal Marines would come pounding onto the scene, round up the slavers and free the slaves. At the time the thought did not seem as melodramatic as it did years later. In 1956 the slavers were sensing the death throes of the British as international policemen, and the slave business was booming.

I am unable to quote prices at the sale I attended but since the end of World War Two many other westerners who have seen slavery at first-hand have evidence of prices and of the existence of slavery, as this sample catalogue shows.

In 1947, Wilfred Thesiger, traveling in Saudi Arabia, quoted the price of a male slave at £75– £112 and that of a girl at £225. With revenue from oil beginning to enrich the many members of the Saudi royal family, prices were going up.[2]

In 1953 the French ambassador to Saudi Arabia reported to his Government that in Jedda a man under forty was bringing £150 at private sales and a girl under fifteen as much as £400.[3]

Dr. Claudie Fayein, who ran a French medical mission in the Yemen in 1955, had more direct contact with slaves than do most westerners. Dr. Fayein was asked to examine a white slave girl and issue a medical certificate that she was a virgin and free from any disease. She was being bought, at £700, as a present for a Saudi prince, a son of King Ibn Saud. The doctor refused to give a certificate and the deal did not go through.[4]

Roderic Owen, a British traveler, noted in 1957: "There is no need to feel satisfied that slavery is a 'dying institution'. The millions in oil royalties have given the industry a new lease of life in Saudi Arabia. Persecution [*sic:* prosecution?] of the slave-traders does not alter the fact that their services are being bought by Saudi Arabian customers, for when there is a demand backed by wealth there will continue to be a supply . . . It [slavery] is criminal in a country which can afford machinery to take the place of slaves."[5]

Lord Maugham visited the Sahara in 1957–8 and bought a 20-year-old male slave from his Tuareg master — "like one buys a piece of meat," as he told the House of Lords. The slave cost Maugham £37.50, and he gave the man his freedom.

In 1959 the Anti-Slavery Society published a report from the English

---

[2] Wilfred Thesiger, *Arabian Sands*. Also, *Anti-Slavery Reporter,* June, 1960.
[3] Report No. 482/AL November 7, 1963, contained in Report No. 75 of the Assembly of the French Union Session 1955– 56. Also, *Anti-Slavery Reporter,* June, 1960.
[4] Claudie Fayein, *A French Doctor in the Yemen*. Also, *Anti-Slavery Reporter,* June, 1960.
[5] Roderic Owen, *The Golden Bubble*.

tutor of a Saudi prince that his employer had paid £2,700 for a Syrian dancing girl, aged thirteen.[6]

In 1960, an Egyptian wife sued her husband in the Egyptian courts and obtained compensation from him for selling her to a Saudi prince. The husband admitted that he had received £3,300 for this wife but that for the other 65 wives he had sold he had received only half this price.[7]

By 1962 — the year in which slavery was officially abolished in Saudi Arabia — prices were still rising; a Saudi Arabian visited the offices of the Anti-Slavery Society to report that a young girl could rarely be bought for less than £3,000 nor a young male for less than £1,000.

In 1963 Saudi Arabia had an estimated 250,000 slaves in a population of six million, according to a *Sunday Telegraph* reporter, but on the eve of the official abolition of slavery prices had fallen.[8] After the decree which banned slavery an underground slave ring began to operate, at even higher prices. Almost limitless revenue from oil was bringing about a resurgence of slavery just as the anti-slavers were jubilant about its end. The Friends World Committee for Consultation — a body recognized by the United Nations — reported the existence of the black market.

The Italian film producer Maleno Malenotti caused a furor in 1965 with his film on modern slavery, especially with his revelation that African Moslems were being tricked into making the great pilgrimage to Islam's holy city, Mecca, where they were sold into slavery.

Malenotti's researches were wide-ranging. He and his film crew went to Darfur and were guided to a house where slaves were sold. The madam of the house displayed a blonde, blue-eyed 14-year-old girl, stripped to the waist. She was said to be the daughter of an English soldier and a colored girl; her price was £500 but, Malenotti was told, to an Arab the price would be £1,000, as the girl was not only a virgin but almost completely white. She was thus doubly desirable.

In Eritrea, hundreds, perhaps thousands of children were fathered by British soldiers during World War Two. Most of them were bought in their teens by wealthy Arabs — up to £800 for a girl and £500 for a boy. Malenotti found many Italian-Ethiopian half-castes, now adults, whose parents had died or been killed during the war. Numbers had been bought in Jibouti by dealers who had reared them until puberty and then sold them to other dealers from Arabia.

Malenotti traced the life of an Italian girl who was sixteen when her settler-parents were killed by the Abyssinians in 1939. In Asmara she was taken over by an elderly female dealer, "Big Mama." This woman sold her for £1,000 to an Egyptian who took the girl to Cairo. Tiring of her after six

[6]*Anti-Slavery Reporter*, June, 1959.
[7]*Trinidad Guardian*, February 28, 1960. *Anti-Slavery Reporter*, June, 1960.
[8]John Osman, *Sunday Telegraph*, March 17 and 24, 1963.

months, he sold her to Mahmoud's Brothel in Khartoum, where she was reserved for select clients. When Malenotti found her she was a street beggar, aged 41 but looking seventy.

In a memorandum of May 18, 1970, the Anti-Slavery Society revealed that "an expatriate administrator employed by the government of a Middle Eastern country" had told the Society that the average annual discrepancy between the number of people entering southern Arabia and the number leaving that region in the same year had been 15,000 over the preceding decade. Allowing for clerical errors, for deaths, for those not counted on leaving and for the obvious fact that many of those missing had entered the region intending to remain, the Society felt that the number of people unaccounted for was larger than it should be. The same official told the Society that in one year — 1966 — at least 300 Somali women were imported into southern Arabia as slaves. In the report, the Society recounted the statement of a bank employee who had seen evidence of his bank's negotiating payment for a consignment of slaves.

In 1971 Dr. Oliver Ransom, who lived and worked in Africa for thirty years, alleged that black children were being auctioned in the Red Sea ports, and in July, 1973, Lord Wilberforce, descendant of the anti-slavery pioneer, cited examples of contemporary slavery in several regions; they included the Sultanate of Muscat and Oman, where slavery had survived under the protection of British arms until 1970.

The same year Mr. Sekyiamah, a member of the United Nations Sub-Commission on Prevention of Discrimination and Protection of Minorities, reported to the Anti-Slavery Society that fifty schoolgirls from his own country, Ghana, had been sold into unpaid service in Lebanon.

In 1979 the Anti-Slavery Society was still agitating for the release of Ndsreen Hussein, a girl kidnapped and subjected to forced marriage in Zanzibar in 1970. She later escaped and was living in Dubai in 1980.

Obviously, from this selection of examples the end of slavery by international and national statute did not mean its end in fact. The Director of the Baptist Union Social Responsibility Office, Don Black, writing in the January, 1975, issue of *The Baptist Times* was challengingly direct: "If you think that slavery went out with Wilberforce you are wrong. Terribly wrong. It didn't. It is still very much alive, with all the horrors of the slave trade."

Paradoxically perhaps, it is easier to conceal the slave trade in the late twentieth century than it was early in the century, for slaves — whatever kind — can now be flown from source to buyer without the possibility of being seen by people who might talk. Also, the once great powers no longer accept the responsibility of suppressing slavery. No machinery exists to implement the United Nations' abolitionist policy; no single U.N. employee has the function of recording instances of slavery. And no government has instructed its U.N. delegates to call for an observer or enforcement organization on anti-slavery. Conditions could hardly be better for slave dealers.

A fundamental favorable condition is money. Some men, with limitless supplies of it, do not stint themselves in anything. Comforts and conveniences can be easily bought — and then people are needed to operate them. With money available it would be easy enough to offer good wages for labor but buying people has a heady attraction of its own. Among such men money itself becomes a plaything with which to buy other playthings. On a trip which took me into Saudi Arabia in 1956 I met a prince — one of many thousands in the Arabian peninsula — who had sent for one of everything in the Sears Roebuck catalogue, possibly the most comprehensive shopping list in the world. But he had tired of unwrapping packages and still had several rooms of parcels. Another prince had solid gold doorknobs and I was told of a gold lavatory chain in Riyadh, the capital of Saudi Arabia.

But throughout history, the first and final requirement of a rich man is service — be it for sexual, commercial, domestic or labor needs. And when there exists a rich society a dealer class will not be far away to fulfill those needs.

In a book which attempts to explain the origins of slavery in Arab lands and its development into an enduring institution it is necessary to define the term "slavery," especially for readers who may have believed the practice to be obsolescent if not obsolete.

The Anti-Slavery Society, whose existence is as important in the late twentieth century as it was when founded (under another name) in 1828, recognizes the definition of slavery given in the League of Nations Slavery Convention of 1926 and repeated in United Nations documents: "Slavery means the status or condition of a person over whom any or all of the powers attached to the right of ownership are exercised."

This is what the Society regards as "chattel slavery." But four other forms of servitude condemned by the United Nations may have many more victims and probably cause overall more misery than chattel slavery. They are debt bondage, serfdom, sham adoption of chlidren, and servile forms of marriage.[9]

Debt bondage occurs when a debtor pledges his own services or those of another person under his control as security for a debt. When he is unable to pay the interest the debtor must surrender himself or some other person, usually the latter, to the money-lender. Bond-servants are usually boys aged nine years or more, but some girls are handed over before the age of puberty.

Serfdom, by definition and by practice, has changed little in centuries. A tenant by law, custom or agreement is bound to live and work on land

---

[9]Forced labor could well be included; it probably causes as much misery as any form of slavery, but it is dealt with by the International Labor Office under its own Convention, and since it is a political phenomenon it is not usually regarded as slavery in the accepted sense.

belonging to another person and to render some determinate service, usually without reward, and is denied any chance to change his status.

Sham adoption of children is widespread. The United Nations defines it this way: "Any institution or practice whereby a child or young person under the age of 18 is delivered by either or both of his natural parents or by his guardian to another person, whether for reward or not, with a view to the exploitation of the child or young person or of his labour."

Three servile forms of marriage are commonplace. (1) A woman, without the right to refuse, is promised or given in marriage on payment of money or goods to her parents, guardian, family or any other person or group. (2) The husband of a woman, his family or clan has the right to transfer her to another person. (3) A woman on the death of her husband is liable to be inherited by another person.

These are somewhat legalistic views of slavery. Other kinds have developed and flourished in recent and modern times. Colonialism, when it was inspired by nothing other than profit and power, was a form of slavery. The Nazis of Germany and the Communists of the Soviet Union evolved a type of infamous and gigantic racial and political slavery. And other nations have sought to hold entire races of people in economic bondage, subjecting hundreds of millions of people to hardships of many kinds. The psychology of this most recent type of slavery is no different from that which underlies the desire of a desert sheikh to dominate a few hundred personal slaves in his palace, harem and gardens. It is the product of history.

"Slaving was in the Arab blood," says Alan Moorehead. "No Arab regarded the trade as any more evil or abnormal than, presumably, a horse-dealer regards as evil or abnormal the buying and selling of horses."

II
The Rites of Slavery

> "Throughout the whole of Islamic history . . . slavery has always been an institution tenacious of life and deeply rooted in custom."
>
> *Encyclopaedia of Islam.*

Arabia has an unbroken tradition of slavery, or *rikk* in Arabic, and to understand the institution in modern times it is necessary to trace the practice of slavery, and attitudes towards it, from the pre-Islamic world to the early part of the nineteenth century.

Before the Prophet Mohammad came to prominence in the year 622 many Arab merchants had grown rich from the slave trade, especially in Mecca, which Mohammad was to establish as Islam's holy city. Most of the slaves — the ordinary Arabic word for slave is *abd* — were Ethiopian, but some white slaves were brought to the area by Arab caravans, some from as far away as south-central Europe. In addition, Arab slaves were part of Arab society — one slave became the adopted son of Mohammad.

The Egyptian kings had owned an inexhaustible supply of slaves with whom they developed the gold and emerald mines of the eastern desert and the turquoise and copper mines of the Sinai. The Egyptians relied mainly on local slave labor and when it was running short (the mortality rate was high) they rounded up tribesmen living along the shores of the Red Sea. Diodorius, a Sicilian historian, says that these slaves were never released from their fetters and were forced to work without rest. "No care is taken of the bodies of these poor creatures . . . they have not a rag to cover their nakedness. For though they are sick, maimed or lame, no rest is allowed them . . . all are driven to work with blows till, overborne with the weight of their misery,

The Rites of Slavery

they drop down dead in the midst of their labours."[1] And all this in shriveling heat, except on winter's nights, which are freezing.

However much they institutionalized slavery, the Arabs cannot be blamed for "inventing" it. It was a constant factor in ancient European, Mediterranean and Middle-Eastern societies, generally in regard to prisoners of war; in the ancient Sumerian language the ideograph for slave meant "slave of a foreign [enemy] land."Rome followed Greece in the use of slaves for hard labor and learned from the Carthaginians their exploitation on a large scale in agriculture. In Italy during the time of Augustus — 63 B.C.E. – 14 C.E. — war was the most commonly used means of meeting the demands of slave markets.

Slavery in Arabia differed from the European version in its acceptance as an institution and the elaborate nature of that institution. Yet Mohammad, through the Koran, did not sanction slavery. At least one world authority on Islam, Eldon Rutter, has said that "the Koran rightly practised would soon bring about a complete cessation of slavery in an Islamic state."[2] Unhappily, he was speaking twelve centuries after Mohammad.

Rutter oversimplifies the teaching of the Koran, which is better summarized by Snouck Hurgronge of Leiden University. "The Law of Islam regulated the position of slaves with much equity. . . . The only legal cause of slavery is prisonership of war or birth from slave parents. . . . According to the Mohammedan principle, slavery is an institution destined to disappear."[3]

Unhappily, this ideal was not carried through, as yet another authority, Bertram Thomas, has explained: "In the abatement of slavery Arabia has been false to her prophet."[4]

Two types of slave were tacitly recognized, the slave bought in normal transaction and the slave born in his master's house, over whom the master had full rights of ownership.(The master was often the father.) In practice, the born-slave was almost certainly safe from being sold or exchanged. Slave owners hired out their female slaves as prostitutes, an ancient custom which, according to some interpretations, was laid down by the Koran, Islam's holy book.

After Mohammad, and despite his teaching, Islam's attitude to the slave was fairly direct. He had to accept the fact of his inferior status and was expected to console himself with the reflection that his soul would enjoy the same eternity as that of a free man. Despite the desperation of the slave's lot, the Koran did hold out some hope for him in this life, since it stresses many times that the freeing of slaves is a meritorious act. More than this, a man

---
[1] *The Historical Library of Diodorius, the Sicilian,* translated by G. Booth.
[2] *The Holy Cities of Arabia*, 1931; also in a lecture to the Royal Asian Society, London, 1933.
[3] *Mohammadanism*. Leiden 1946.
[4] *The Arabs,* London, 1938.

could gain direct benefits by freeing a slave. For instance, he could atone for certain crimes, including the causing of accidental death; a perjurer could be absolved if he freed a slave.

The Koran stated that nobody could lawfully have sexual intercourse with female slaves except their masters, or their husbands, except if one of these gave his consent. A slave, male or female, could legally marry. Masters of slaves were advised, under Koranic law, to see that deserving slaves *did* marry. It was even permissible for Moslem slaves to marry free Moslems, and a Moslem slave woman, on marriage, was entitled to a dowry from her husband. Koranic tradition instructs masters not to show contempt for their slaves. In practice, this meant calling him by some euphemism, such as "my servant." He was supposed to treat the slave humanely, to feed and clothe him adequately, not to overwork him, to forgive his faults. If after all this the master could not live in harmony with his slave, he was to sell him to another master.

It was always open to a master to free his slave; for religious reasons this was almost obligatory when he had treated him harshly or brutally. A happy augury was to free a slave at the time of an eclipse; this particular freeing could atone for breaking the fast of Ramadan. The spiritual rewards for freeing a slave were enormous, as one of the best-known hadiths[5] ordained: "God will free from hell the man who frees a Moslem slave." God would also smile on the master who educated a slave girl, freed her and married her. Of course, all these benefits were available only in relation to Moslem slaves; it was not necessary to be so humane to unbelievers.

As slavery became more institutionalized, Moslem law noted that slavery was justified by only two means — capture in war or birth in slavery. Capture in war did not affect Moslems; in this situation they could not be reduced to slavery.

Because of the stipulation concerning the source of slaves they were in short supply in the era after Mohammad. The supply could be replenished only by those non-Moslems captured in war or imported commercially. But there was a way around the difficulty. The Arab tribe or race needing slaves would declare jihad [holy war] and was thus legally entitled to seize the civilian inhabitants of any captured town in foreign territory. Slavery was, therefore, one of the principal causes of war. All this made nonsense of the Moslem jurists' principle that liberty was the root of their faith.

Whatever the moralistic teaching of the Koran and the hadiths, the slave was a commodity, a chattel. In an Arab home he had no more rights than the family animals; the new-born slave — that is, the infant born to a slave mother by a master — was wholly the man's property and the mother had no rights of maternity.

---

[5] Beliefs not in the Koran itself but hallowed by Islamic tradition.

It was possible for a slave to belong jointly to two masters, a situation fraught with complexity. Customs varied from tribe to tribe. In some regions, the buyer of a slave held him on approval for three days; if in that time he had not detected any physical or personality flaws in the slave he was required to pay up. Should the slave become mad or develop leprosy within a year the master could demand a refund from the seller.

A complex system of regulations, prohibitions, entitlements and prices grew up around the institution, so that a female slave with whom the master intended to cohabit would cost more than an ordinary woman whom he might take for his pleasure but who was intended more as a servant. He might try to circumvent this qualification by declaring that some highly desirable woman he was buying was meant merely to be a drudge, but should he then live with her he would soon be found out and his reputation would suffer. In other Arab regions, non-Moslems could not keep slaves; they had to free them or sell them, generally at low prices, to a Moslem. Another law stated that if a master did not adequately feed and clothe his slave or if he beat him to the point of mutilation, the slave could be sold by the Law. But who was likely to report the brutal master? And what constituted mutilation? A slave flogged in places where his wounds were covered by his clothing could not expect the Law to save him from his master.

The slave did have a few things in his favor. As a slave he was unable to exercise free will; so he was not obligated to attend Friday prayers, go on pilgrimages and fight in Holy Wars. The Moslem slave-woman had rather more latitude about showing her "nakedness" — revealing her face and arms — than the free woman.

Any potential threat posed by intelligent slaves was removed by forbidding them to hold the position of religious magistrate, though many did lead their local congregations in prayer.

The rights of the slave might seem fairly comprehensive but in practice they were subject to approval by the master. For instance, while the adult male slave might marry of his own accord, he needed his master's approval of the woman he chose. The master was also guardian of all his female slaves; so he could easily forbid any one of them from continuing to see a man who was courting her. Similarly, the master could insist on either a male or female slave marrying a person of the master's choice. One right the slave husband did share with the free man — he could divorce his wife as he wished.

Under Koranic law, divorced women or widows are not permitted to have sexual relations with a man for stated periods — four months and ten days for a widow. A slave woman widow could halve this period of withdrawal. A divorced woman had to "withdraw" for three menstrual or intermenstrual periods; the slave woman need withdraw for only two. These "privileges" were, however, not conceived out of a desire to be fair to the woman but to make her more rapidly available to men.

Legal concubinage, as it affected slaves, was complex enough to form social attitudes which have endured for centuries. The Koran permits a married man to cohabit only with his own female slave, though in most Arab societies nobody was likely to be critical of a man who tried out a slave belonging to his son. But he was absolutely forbidden to cohabit with a slave belonging to his wife, even with his wife's consent. Co-owners of a female slave could not cohabit with her at the same time and the sole owner of a married female slave could not cohabit with her, though this rule was often breached. Any concubine was pleased to have a child by her master because this gave her immense security: she could not afterwards be sold, and on her master's death she was automatically free.

A free man could have a maximum of four wives but the number of his concubines was unlimited; he was limited only by the traditional prohibitions — he could not cohabit with a woman of natural or acquired kinship, with two sisters together or with a woman professing a heathen religion.

In a society so promiscuous, parentage was often a problem. Who was to say which man was the father of a child born to a slave woman who had been sold two or three times in rapid succession; or, similarly, to a slave woman who had been married. Islamic law stated that she must not be taken in sexual intercourse for one menstrual period, that is, until her non-pregnancy was clear. If she was pregnant, then the ban lasted until her confinement. If she was not yet regular in her periods or had ceased to be regular, the period was one to three months, according to the ruling of the jurists of the particular race.

Paternity problems became hopelessly involved, sometimes to the point where the child, at puberty, was allowed to choose his father from the two or more possibilities. One tribe preferred a two-fold paternity as the most rational solution to an irrational situation.

Most schools of Islamic thought allow the master to do as he wishes with property in possession of his slave; anything the slave has or anything he might earn or acquire is entirely the master's. These profits could be great, for some masters have given clever slaves charge of a business or have trusted them with large sums on trading missions to distant places.

In many parts of Arabia slaves were branded with their master's mark of ownership. In some societies this was the work of the barber, who shaved the slave's head and then cut or burnt the mark into the slave's cheek or forehead. When a slave changed hands his slave-mark was changed or effaced, and this too was part of the barber's daily work. A slave who had escaped might try to persuade the barber to alter his mark, but a barber risked having his hand cut off for this offense. A runaway slave who denied his master when identified by him could, in some regions, lose an ear in punishment.

Punishment for slaves was reckoned according to another complex formula. Some punishments were the same as for a free man — for example, cutting off the hand for theft, and death for apostasy. Fornication did not legally involve the death penalty, but fifty lashes could be inflicted, sometimes along with banishment. The slave guilty of a false charge of fornication against a free person could be given forty lashes, but as the victim of such a slander he could expect no redress.

Once a master announced that he planned to free a slave he could not revoke this emancipation; however he could insure against any doubt he might have by saying that the freeing was to take place at some future date. In this case the slave could be sold before the waiting period expired, thus nullifying the emancipation. The slave held in joint ownership was in a difficult situation if one owner wanted to free him and the other did not. Generally, the outcome was that he was still owned but by fewer masters.

For many centuries it was possible for a slave to ransom himself, generally by spaced-out payments laid down by contract. Obviously, to make this money the slave was authorized by his master to engage in business. Theoretically a female slave could free herself by ransom; in practice she was rarely allowed to do so since, being a woman, she might sell herself to get the necessary money.

The slave freed by self-ransom could sometimes depend on a small bonus payment. However he gained his liberty, the freed slave had the same legal rights as any freeborn man, with the significant condition that both he and his male descendants would remain forever attached to his former master or mistress and to their family; that is, as an employee in their service.

The child born in wedlock did not follow the status of his mother, bond or free, but was born free if either of his parents was free. The master of a female slave could grant a third party the use of her, for purposes of work or sexual relations.

Wars provided many slaves. Arab marauders constantly raided deep into enemy territory — and any non-Moslem territory was enemy — to find captives. The Christian seaboard of the Mediterranean was particularly vulnerable, and many innocent farmers, fishermen and their families were seized.

Sometimes Moslems made slaves of other Moslems, for instance when the members of fanatical Islamic sects attacked those they regarded as weak followers of Islam and worth little more regard than Christians. In the year 1077 thousands of women of a Berber tribe — an Arab group — were sold at public sales in Cairo.

As Islam spread into Negro Africa, the slavers were not far behind, and many pagan children joined the markets in Arabia and Morocco. Slaves were regarded as nothing more than a commodity of trade, and slavers' caravans penetrated deeply into Africa and Asia on long expeditions. Slavers' ships probed the Mediterranean, the Black Sea and the Red Sea. Negroes, Ethiopians, Berbers, Turks, Slavs, Spaniards — all were picked up by the thousands. During one long period beginning in the eighth century the Venetians became slavers and formed the last link in a slave chain which stretched deep into western Europe.

The traffic was immense, with slave compounds at Almeria in Spain, Alexandria and Farame in Egypt, Darband on the Caspian and at Taranto, Italy. In the Moslem world every big town had its slave market, and this was sometimes an enormous place with many private display rooms, shops, alleys and houses. The slavers lived within this market, always in luxury and sometimes in opulence. Cunning men, the slavers exploited both their slaves and their clients. They knew how to conceal age and infirmity and how to exaggerate muscles and breasts. Some used dye to darken grey hair or wigs to provide more allure.

Desirable girls and women were perfumed and oiled to make them even more desirable; weak men were given drugs which enabled them to lift heavy weights when ordered by the dealer to perform for a potential customer. Unsightly scars were painted over. Light and shade deftly used in the inspection room deceived many a buyer into paying much more than normal market prices.

The researchers of the *Encyclopaedia of Islam* record that in eleventh century Spain Berbers were preferred to Catalans and Galicians. At Alexandria in the fifteenth century, the order of preference was Tartars, Circassions, Greeks, Serbs and Albanians. Among women, Berbers were considered best for housework, sexual relations and childbearing; Greek women could be trusted to look after valuable property; Negresses were docile, if not particularly intelligent; Armenians and Indians were difficult to manage and did not make tractable slaves.

In Persia [Iran] many white slaves came from the Malabar coast of India and were highly prized as intelligent and good-looking. Caucasian girls were favorites for the harems. With some poetic justice, many Persians themselves became slaves. Almost constantly at war with the people of Turkestan, the Persian armies lost many soldiers captured by the enemy. They were sold in thousands at the great slave market of Bokhara, often in lots according to age or height or assessment of muscle-power.

Gratification of the owner's pleasures was the principal reason for purchase of female slaves — and still is. But the rich Arab was also conscious of his friends' pleasure and would often train a favorite female slave to play a musical instrument to entertain them. The highly professional slave dealer would sometimes give his women slaves long and special training in sexual behavior to increase their value.

While many male slaves spent their lives in their owner's gardens or tending his flocks, as many others were trained as personal bodyguards or as soldiers for some prince or ruler. Hence tall, powerful men brought good prices. Agents for a wealthy ruler might buy hundreds of slaves at a single sale and the profit to the dealer was immense.

The military aspect of slavery is a phenomenon peculiar to the Middle-Eastern Islam. From the first Arab conquests, military guards and vast Negro and white militias were made up of slaves; the armed slave replaced the Arab, Berber or Iranian soldier. The military strength of the Ottoman Empire depended on the slave battalions — Janissaries or Mamelukes — recruited from the white children stolen from Christian families in Eastern Europe, the Balkans and Slav countries, sold in the big markets of the Ottoman Empire and transported to special barracks to devote their lives to the service of the Sultan.

The Mamelukes were not wiped out in Egypt until the beginning of the nineteenth century, following the intervention of Napoleon and the repressions of Mohammad Ali, who immediately established huge barracks in Upper Egypt in order to hold captured black Sudanese to serve in his army.

Eunuchs were prominent in the palaces of all nobles and of any ordinary Moslem able to afford a harem. Since castration was necessary to turn a man into a eunuch, obviously few volunteers were forthcoming. The Arabs had two types of castration operations — one for whites and another for blacks. Simply put, the whites were given extra care and left with some penis; many could still perform coitus and some took concubines. The blacks were the victims of a brutal, bloody and often lethal operation which left them, as it was said, "level with the abdomen." The difference in treatment was based on the assumption that the blacks had an ungovernable sexual appetite. In most cases the operation was carried out forcibly by knocking the victim unconscious or by tying him down.

The high death rate castration caused among slaves explains somewhat the great demand for black slaves during the centuries. It also explains the high price paid for a Negro slave, castrated and still in good condition. Many slave dealers did not leave the slaves to be castrated by the buyer but maintained their own surgeon to do the job. This was not inspired by any humanitarianism; it was a simple fact that a eunuch slave in good health was worth more than any other type. Some eunuchs prospered and became masters of harems, teachers and respected advisers to their owners.

It would be wrong to suppose that most slaves spent their lives shackled by chains or constantly watched by alert overseers armed with whips. Such extreme steps were hardly necessary in Arabia; the trackless, waterless deserts took the place of chains and guards. In any case, a runaway slave who was physically different from the Arabs in color, features and build was easily recognized. He had very few places in which to hide, unlike a black slave in the Americas, who could hide in forest and swamp, in the mountains or in the large towns.

Because no constant watch was necessary on slaves, many served as assistants in business, or even carried on business themselves. Some had considerable independence — provided they furthered their master's interests.

Again, the use of large gangs of slaves to build public roads, reservoirs or fortifications was rare. The roads had been in existence for centuries and nobody contemplated a road-building program, while the concept of public works was alien to Arab society. When a mass of workers was needed for some great project, such as a bridge, prisoners of war were used. They had cost nothing and their lives were of no importance; slaves had cost money and must be kept alive, if sometimes only just alive.[6]

Despite the perils of desert and heat, the probability of dying of thirst and the certainty of punishment if caught, many slaves did run away. Often this was the result of homesickness or sexual deprivation and was a form of desperate protest rather than a reasoned plan of escape. The number of successful escapes throughout Arabia's many centuries of slavery must be very small.

Those Europeans who had been captured in war or seized in an Arab foray on a foreign coast had greater hope of salvation. Their own country or town or tribe might try to exchange them for prisoners, or ransom them for cash or jewels. Christian groups often considered the recovery of their people from Moslem hands a sacred and moral duty. Wealthy Catholic orders spent vast sums of money on these attempts, possibly too much money, because the Arab raiders realized that they could sometimes gain more in the ransom of slaves than in an ordinary sale. The negotiators were, in most cases, Jewish businessmen and travelers who were trusted by both sides.

Slavery had a profound influence on Moslem society in a way that seems to have been little considered. Freed slaves rarely returned to their homelands — the sheer physical difficulties saw to that — and so they mingled with the native Moslems. Inter-breeding was commonplace, with considerable ethnological results. The slave population of some cities was sometimes as much as thirty per cent, with consequent cultural blendings.

Many people profited from the slave trade and not least the "authorities" — princes, rulers of all kinds and the equivalent of councils and cabinets. Most of them taxed the money spent on slaves, not infrequently exacting money from the seller *and* the buyer. Despite the many tax evasions, profits were considerable.

After the Moslem Moors were driven from Spain late in the fifteenth century, Iberia was no longer the fruitful slavehunting ground it had been. Not that this reduced the number of Christian slaves; the enterprise and vigor

---

[6]History records exceptions. In the ninth century large numbers of East African slaves were taken to Mesopotamia to reclaim fearsome swamp lands for cultivation. These slaves revolted and were mercilessly hunted down and slaughtered.

of the Barbary pirates, operating from the North African coast, produced excellent slave cargoes, notably in the seventeenth century. The corsairs picked up many a merchant vessel in the Atlantic and Mediterranean and grew rich on the human spoils. So lucrative was the trade that the Barbary chieftains even sent salesmen to Arabia to secure firm orders for slaves of various types. Other representatives were sent into Europe to negotiate ransoms. Here, as elsewhere, Jews acted as ransom negotiators, often risking their lives to bring captives to freedom.

Generally, the pirates treated their rich, well-born captives very well — at least for as long as a ransom seemed possible. The ordinary slaves — the crews of captured ships, soldiers, servants — were put to work at oars in a Barbary galley or had their physiques developed in farm work or heavy labor until a buyer was found for them. Because it was easier to escape in northwest Africa than in the Arabian peninsula large groups of slaves were kept chained; all were guarded and locked up at night.

Barbary strongholds such as Algiers made as much money from slaves as from captured property. At times as many as thirty thousand slaves lived in Algiers — a vast human stock from which orders were filled with efficiency, skill and absolute coldbloodedness.

In the seventeenth century even England was not safe from Arab slavers' raids. Between 1609 and 1616, one period for which records exist, Barbary corsairs, with a fleet of 100 ships, captured 466 British vessels and enslaved their crews and passengers. But the slavers were still bolder. One Sunday in 1640 they raided a village near Penzance while the bulk of the population was at prayer in church, rounded up the whole congregation of sixty and carried them off to slavery.

The worst raid by Barbary corsairs in the British Isles was the sack of Baltimore, a small fishing village in southwest Ireland. Piloted by an Irish traitor, the Arabs sailed into the little harbor by night, burned the town and abducted 273 Irish men, women and children.

Slave raiding increased so much in the west of England that townsfolk as well as coastal villagers pleaded that the Lizard navigation light be extinguished because it helped the corsairs. The Barbary port of Salee was such a menace to England that a naval squadron under Captain William Rainsborow blockaded the port, battering the fortifications and destroying any ship which attempted to leave. Unfortunately the squadron was recalled, and by 1640 the slavers were as bold as ever. That year they attacked the frigate *Elizabeth* off the Lizard and burned her, occupied the Scilly Isles, landed at Fowey and enslaved 240 people, including several ladies of quality. And at least one slaver sailed twenty miles up the Thames to find women for Turkish harems.

In 1652 the frigate *Speaker* was sent to Algiers with £30,000 to ransom English captives, paying £1,100 for Alice Hayes and £800 for Sarah

Ripley of London, who had been sold for £38 in the slave market five years before.

These two women and others ransomed with them were fortunate. At this time the corsairs held more than 5,000 English men, women and children among the 30,000 white Christian slaves working in their homes, streets and quarries. At least 1,500 English slaves were maintained in Salee, all captured in raids on the English coast within twenty miles of Dartmouth, Falmouth or Plymouth.

The corsairs did not leave England alone until Admiral Blake bombarded Tunis and terrified Algiers.

Unfortunate Christians, most of them European, were moved in and out of North African ports until the 1830s, when the French began their imperial conquest in Africa. But the traffic in Negroes from the North African ports did not slacken. Morocco was a leading slaver nation of this area, and since the French could not prevent slavery they connived at it. In response to public opinion they closed the more open slave markets at Fez and Rabat and blocked the notorious route from Timbuktu, but their army was never large enough to do more than inconvenience the Arab slavers operating from Central Africa. David Livingstone described the region, in his last words, as "this open sore of the world."

After this summary of the general Arab practice of slavery — we will later examine Islam's attitude to the institution — we will probe various parts of the "open sore," which was infinitely more gross than even Livingstone could have imagined.

III
The Exploitation of East Africa

In Africa, the Arabs have always thought themselves to be in a land of conquest; so it is odd that Arab occupation of parts of the African continent has been given scant attention in the history of the colonial partition of Africa.

One reads of the Arab invasions of North Africa in the seventh and twelfth centuries; Arab penetration along the East African coast and conflict between the Arabs settled at Zanzibar and the English, but the Arabs who conquered East Africa have never been considered colonizers by most historians.

The explanation is partly that Islam conquered the northern and eastern coasts of Africa in a religious context, but mainly that colonization is considered a phenomenom of white races, and Europeans in particular. This opinion probably has its psychological root in the fact that military and political conquest are prime facets of colonialism. But the Arabs, conquerors of the Africans whom they subjugated for centuries, were in their turn subjects of European colonial supremacy. If colonialism means, as it generally does, the forceful conquest and exploitation of one nation by another, the keeping of others in a socially, culturally, economically and racially inferior state, then the Arabs cannot be omitted from the list of colonizing powers, because they too dominated, exploited and divided Africa in the nineteenth century. Indeed, chronologically they are at the head of the list — by about 1,200 years. The Arab colonization of the East African coastlands began about the year 700. Arab connection with the coast and with the slave trade is a further 600 years old. Our earliest description of Africa, the Greek *Periplus* or guide for navigators, tells of Arabs trading down the coast and "slaves of the better sort" being exported from Somaliland to Egypt. After real colonization began, a steady supply of slaves was obtained from the African interior, both for domestic use of the Arab colonists and also, and in greater volume as time went on, for export to Arabia, Iraq, Persia and India.

Along the southern East African coast, too, Arab dhows were engaged in a continual hunt for slaves to satisfy the growing markets in Madagascar and the Comorro Islands. Contemporary observers, such as Captain W.F. Owen R.N., could not then even guess at the volume of the slave trade along the coast of what is now northern Mozambique. Some native peoples, such as the Yao and Makua, were engaged in slavery, but the Arabs gradually squeezed them out by the simple process of taking the native slavers themselves as slaves.

The slave traffic in East Africa, by land and sea, assumed vast proportions after Sa'id, the Prince of Muscat, gained an even stronger hold on the coast of Africa at the beginning of the nineteenth century. The British persistently opposed slavery, and between 1812 and 1822 English diplomats on the coast parleyed continually with Sa'id. That decade of hard work resulted only in Sa'id's forbidding his Arabs to export slaves outside the shipping lane joining Africa to Arabia. This was practically worthless, since Sa'id insisted on the lawfulness of slave traffic within African territory and on the import of slaves. For most of another century countless wretched Africans were enslaved and sold.

During the nineteenth century — and we are mainly concerned here with the nineteenth and twentieth centuries — there was a general Moslem expansionism inside Africa, though the Arabs from Oman had been progressively infiltrating since the sixteenth century into the areas from Muscat to the Comorro Islands. So strongly were they established along the east coast of Africa that in the seventeenth century the Sultan of Oman transferred his capital to the island of Zanzibar, which became the main slave market throughout the nineteenth century, in spite of English efforts to stop the trade.

Zanzibar was a great slave entrepôt. Gathered from much of Central Africa, thousands of men and women were sold to the Arabs and Indians who owned the clove plantations and sugar estates along the East African coast and in Zanzibar itself. In the fierce, humid climate they were worked beyond their natural capacity and many died or had their health so ruined that their masters threw them out. These particular slaves obviously had no particular graces or accomplishments, or they would have been sold at higher prices to more considerate owners.

In 1811, Captain Smee of the Royal Navy, giving a detailed account of his visit to Zanzibar, estimated that 6,000–10,000 slaves were exported annually by Arabs to Muscat, India and the Mascarene Islands.

Smee's description of the slave market is probably the most vivid on record.

> The show commences about four o'clock in the afternoon. The slaves, set off to the best advantage by having the skins cleaned and burnished with cocoanut oil, their faces painted with red and white stripes, which is here esteemed elegance, and the hands, noses, ears, and feet ornamented with a profusion of bracelets of gold and silver and jewels are ranged in a line, commencing with the youngest, and increasing to the rear according to their size and age. At the head of this file, which is composed of all sexes [sic] and ages from 6 to 60, walks the person who owns them; behind . . . is the guard. . . . When any of them strikes a spectator's fancy the line immediately stops and an examination ensues which is unequalled in any cattle market in Europe. The intending purchaser . . .examines the person, the mouth and the feet first and every part of the body in procession, not even excepting the breasts etc. of the girls, many of whom I have seen handled in the most indecent manner . . . there is every reason to believe that the slave-dealers force the young girls to submit to their lust previous to their being disposed of . . . I have frequently counted between twenty and thirty of these files in the market. Women with children newly born hanging at their breasts and others so old they can scarcely walk, are sometimes dragged about in this manner. . . . From such scenes one turns away in pity and indignation. . . . [From R. Coupland, *East Africa's Invaders.*]

In 1818, the introduction of the cultivation of cloves marked an economic revolution in Zanzibar. The Arabs took possession of all cultivable land and the native Negro population withdrew to the north, afraid of being made to work in servile conditions for the new masters of the land. The planters then had to turn to the African hinterland to find their labor.

African slavery was already an ancient institution, but it gained a new impetus from the demands of the Zanzibar and Pemba farmers. Thus the Arabs became established not only as a class of merchants and administrators, but as an aristocracy of planters whose interests were vitally linked to the preservation of the slave trade.

The Arab advance into the interior was encouraged by the import of low-price firearms by Sa'id. Zanzibar became an important port under this Prince, and a great market for slaves, ivory, cloves, rubber and copal. On the coast, the new ports of Bagamyyo, Sadania and Pangami were departure points for the routes to the great lakes — Victoria, Nyasa and Tanganyika — where the Arabs arrived about 1840. Permanent relay stations were set up, of which Kazeh was the most important; here the route forked to the regions of Muanza and Ujiji on the two lakes. Some Arabs did the actual slave capturing; others were specialists in "grouping" and exporting slaves and ivory. "On the coast," says Trimingham, "the economy was based on slavery . . . in the last century the Arabs' prosperity was largely based on the slaves' work in plantations under the control of administrators. The artisans, servants, sailors, team-leaders were all slaves."

In 1846, the English decision to abolish the preferential price of sugar — thus establishing a "free" market — created an enormous demand for slaves to work in Brazil's plantations. They were captured mainly in the Portuguese regions of East Africa, but Zanzibar gained most from this trade, serving as an embarkation port.

The explorer Richard Burton describes the life led by the Arabs on the slave route, at Unyanyembe, in the 1850s. "The Arabs lived comfortably, even splendidly . . . surrounded by troups of concubines and slaves which they destined for different trades and occupations."

Burton and Speke on their expedition in 1857–1859 passed huge slave caravans, some of them 1,000 strong, and saw the human wreckage in their wake.

The Arab slave-merchants had established depots of provisions and arms, and at first maintained a distinction (which was to disappear later) between the ivory and slave routes. The slaves usually followed the Lake Nyasa–Kilwa route. The restrictions of the slave trade imposed on the Sultan of Zanzibar, Bargash, by the English Consul, John Kirk, caused an economic crisis in the town of Kilwa, which was earning up to £120,000 profit from slaves.

But to discuss slave trading in economic, ethical or any other dispassionate and academic terms is to miss the point. This was a trade in human misery and degradation not to be equaled until the excesses of Nazi Germany and Stalinist Russia. The sheer horror of the trade was reported in detail by many reliable witnesses — explorers, missionaries, ships' captains, consuls, doctors.

To understand fully the slaves' plight it is necessary to look at the long and terrible journey overland and at the shorter but even more horrifying crossing from Kilwa to Zanzibar.

First came the assault on villages. They were set on fire, cattle were driven off, and often standing crops were cut down. Nobody was left to cultivate them unless a handful of fugitives crept back to the wreckage — the smoking huts, the blackened ground strewn with broken household goods and bits of furniture, the unburied dead. This destruction was so widespread that explorers speak of "miles of ruined villages." When raids occurred in the growing season the anarchy they caused meant insufficient crops — and famine. That in turn increased the slave trade, for a starving tribe would sell some of its own people for food. David Livingstone knew of chiefs, facing starvation, who sold children aged from eight to ten years "for less corn than would go into one of our hats."

Livingstone often crossed the slavers' paths and wherever a caravan had passed the evidence of devastation and cruelty enraged him. He describes many instances of men, women and children who had been killed or left tied to a tree for the scavengers to finish off when they were too ill, exhausted or starved to keep up with the caravan. Mostly, Livingstone tells us, they were finished off with a blow from a rifle butt or the skull was smashed with a rock. This happened to a child whose mother complained that she could not manage both the child and the heavy ivory tusk the slavers expected her to carry to the coast. Sometimes, if the Arabs did not have enough of their own kind to drive and guard the slaves, they used *wangwans*-armed and freed slaves who were quite as cruel as their masters, since their own lives depended on their "efficiency."

A caravan could be made up of a few dozen slaves or thousands, at least in the jungle, but the order of march was much the same for all caravans in regions where the victims might escape. They were roped or chained together in gangs with hands tied behind their backs; if they were "difficult," they had a piece of wood tied into their mouths. If a man tried to escape his neck was secured into a cleft stick as thick as a man's thigh and locked by a crossbar. Sometimes a double cleft stick was used with a man locked into either end. The women were usually roped together by the neck and the children came trailing behind.

At all points on their way inland and back again the traders were anxious to pick up slaves, if only in twos and threes. Kidnapping of natives by natives was rife along the main routes for, as Livingstone wrote, "the Arabs buy whoever is brought to them." Victims were sometimes caught while walking in the bush quite close to their villages.

Not an aspect of slavery escaped Livingstone. From a native village he wrote," . . . . Slaves are sold here in the same open way that the business is carried on in a Zanzibar slave-market. A man goes about calling out the price he wants for a slave, who walks behind him; if a woman she is taken into a hut to be examined in a state of nudity. . . . Slavery is a great evil wherever I have seen it. A poor woman and child are among the captives, the boy about three years old seems a mother's pet. His feet are sore from walking in the sun. He was offered for two fathoms and his mother for one fathom; he understood it all, and cried bitterly, clinging to his mother. She had, of course, no power to help him; they were separated . . . [This] is an episode of everyday occurrence in the wake of a slave trader. Two fathoms, mentioned as the price of the boy's life — the more valuable of the two — means four yards of unbleached calico. . . . The reader must not think that there are no lower prices . . . boys and girls are sometimes to be bought for a few handfuls of maize."

Another principal witness of slavery was the missionary-mariner Alfred J. Swann, employed by the London Missionary Society to run the first mission boat on Lake Tanganyika. A determined man, Swann wrote, "In the midst of the Arabs' vile operations it was our fixed determination to live, and in time, to undermine or destroy their diabolical trade in human souls and bodies."

He had not at that time seen slaves but he was soon to encounter a caravan owned by the "great" slaver, Hamed bin Mohammad, known to history as Tippu Tip, and he was horrified. "As they filed past we noticed many chained by the neck. Others had their neck fastened into the forks of poles . . . . The women . . . carried babies on their back in addition to a tusk of ivory or other burden on their heads. They looked at us with suspicion, having been told . . . that white men always desired the release of slaves in order to eat their flesh . . . It is difficult to describe the filthy state of their bodies; in many instances not only scarred by the cut of a chikote [the hide whip] but feet and shoulders were a mass of open sores, made more painful by the swarms of flies which . . . lived on the flowing blood. They presented a moving picture of utter misery and one could not help wondering how many had survived the long tramp from the Upper Congo, at least 1,000 miles distant. Our own inconveniences sank into insignificance compared with the suffering of this crowd of half-starved, ill-treated creatures who, weary and friendless, must have longed for death."

Swann asked a headman slaver what happened when slaves became too ill to travel. "Spear them at once," he said. "If we did not, then others would pretend that they were ill in order to avoid carrying their loads. . . . We never leave them alive on the road; they all know our custom."[1]

Like Livingstone decades earlier, Swann was furious—"every humane feeling within me rose in rebellion"— but like Livingstone he was unable to help except to send indignant protests to Zanzibar and England.

Those slaves who survived the trek and who were not being taken even further overland were then stowed on dhows bound for Zanzibar. The use of the word "stowed" is deliberate. The dhows were lightly built sailing boats, occasionally partly decked but usually quite open, and weighing eighty tons. When engaged in slaving, these vessels had temporary platforms of bamboo, leaving a narrow passage in the center. The Negroes were stowed in bulk, the first layer along the floor of the vessel, two adults side by side with a boy or girl resting between or on them, until the tier was complete. Over them the first platform was laid, supported an inch or two clear of their bodies; then a second, third and fourth tier were laid until they reached the gunwale of the dhow.[2] Here the slaves remained for at least three days. Those who did not die from asphyxia were often struck by cholera.[3]

---

[1] Alfred J. Swann, *Fighting the Slave Hunters in Central Africa.*
[2] Details of this stowage are given by Captain Moresby in Captain Smee's *East Africa and Its Invaders;* by Captain Sullivan, R.N., who drew sketches to show the method of packing; by Dr. Steere who lived in Zanzibar and several others who witnessed dhow slave-loading.
[3] Burton states that cholera in India was "nothing" compared with the epidemics in Kilwa. In 1870, two hundred slaves died daily and the price dropped radically for fear of contagion.

HMS Daphne (Captain Sullivan) caught a dhow with 156 slaves off the Somali coast. Sullivan reported: "On the bottom on the dhow was a pile of stones as ballast and on these stones, without even a mat, were 23 women huddled together, a few with infants in their arms. These women were literally doubled up, there being no room to sit erect. On a bamboo deck, about three feet above the keel, were 48 men, crowded together in the same way; and on another deck above this were 53 children. Some of the slaves were in the last stages of starvation and dysentery. On getting the vessel alongside and clearing her out, a woman came up having an infant about a month or six weeks old in her arms with its forehead crushed in. She told us that just before out boat came alongside the dhow the child began to cry and one of the Arabs, fearing the English would hear it, took up a stone and struck it."

The Royal Navy's anti-slavery patrols failed largely because seven or eight ships were not enough to blockade 4,000 miles of coast; between 1867 – 1869 it was roughly estimated that while 2,645 smuggled slaves were caught and freed, about 37,000 were passed through to Arabia.

Sullivan described the stratagems employed by Arab merchants to escape British control. The most common ploy was to load the boat with legal merchandise; then to take one or more slaves on board at each stopping-place. Thus their numbers increased as the destination, usually Zanzibar, was reached, so reducing the risk of arrest by the Royal Navy. "It was common practice," says the naval captain, "for Arab passengers boarding the boats to use the slave servants they brought with them as payment for their passage."

To escape British control, the Arabs used to dress the women slaves as sailors' wives and put motley-colored turbans on the men slaves to make them appear ordinary passengers. When the captain of a slave dhow risked a direct voyage, he loaded the vessel heavily, resulting in the suffocation of many of the slaves; in these overcrowded small craft the temperature at sea reached 35 degrees centigrade.

British attempts to control the trade increased the hardships of the slaves. Prices were going up and it paid the dealer to cram more and more of his victims into the dhows; if just one vessel in four got through it was enough to make a profit. Richard Burton reported that the dhows were now built "with 18 inches between the decks, one pint of water was served out per diem and five wretches were stowed away instead of two."

Natives were sometimes enticed aboard a dhow with a bottle of rum or a decoy girl and then clapped under hatches.

Burton's description of the Zanzibar market in 1856 shows how little conditions had changed for the better since Smee's day. "Lines of negroes stood out like beasts, the broker calling out [a description of his wares]. The least hideous of the black faces were surmounted by scarlet night-caps. All were horribly thin with ribs protruding like the circles of a cask, and not a few squatted sick on the ground. . . ."

At this time about 5,500 Arabs lived in Zanzibar; some of them owned as many as 2,000 slaves in addition to large plantations of cloves and coconut-palms, three-story wooden houses with fine carved doorways and wardrobes of rich clothing.

The demand was enormous, and between 20,000 and 40,000 slaves were imported into the Zanzibar market every year. Of the slaves actually working in Zanzibar about thirty per cent of the males died of disease and malnutrition every year and had to be replaced, thus maintaining the trade's impetus.

Like the Europeans, the Arabs in the nineteenth century were conquerors of vast African territories from which they gained considerable economic advantage, exploiting men and squandering local wealth. They were not able to establish a lasting local administration because of the arrival of the Europeans, but this did not prevent them from maintaining, long after the partition of Africa, zones of influence or, rather, hunting zones from which they drew enormous profits until the struggle of European powers against slavery put an end to them.

Arab expansionism was based on such Arabized coastal towns as Mombasa, which were subject to the sovereignty of the Sultans of Oman. Until the nineteenth century the Arabs in this region had been content to seize black slaves for their own needs. But from 1860 they became the main providers of human contraband for America, and monopolized the ivory trade.

The European conquest of Asia and in particular the Far East had created the fashion in Europe for objects and furniture inlaid with ivory. The price of ivory depended largely on the cost of its transport from the interior; so the use of slaves as porters became one of the main sources of profit for the Arab merchants. Keltie, in *The Partition of Africa,* thinks that for every slave the Arabs bought to the coast, at least six died on the way or upon capture. The supply being virtually unlimited, such losses were accepted . The slave merchants were so well-organized that on several occasions they were victorious in armed clashes with the British who, as they extended their influence across Africa, brought with them the suppression of slavery.

The British sent Sir Bartle Frere to negotiate with Bargash, the Sultan of Zanzibar and son of Sa'id, and in 1873 Bargash, in a treaty agreed with Britain, prohibited the maritime slave traffic and public slave markets.

The treaty meant little, for the forbidden sea route was quickly replaced by a new land route and the number of slaves did not decrease though the mortality was higher. A British agent, Holmwood, put the number smuggled by the new route between October, 1873, and October, 1874, at 15,000. Slaves were sold in the bigger towns right along this route, the last of them in Somalia. "Beyond Malindi," Holmwood reported, "the mortality begins to increase so rapidly that every hour is important." Naturally, the further north, the higher the price. "The new land route," he said "is admitted by all to be a paying venture . . . next year's exports are expected to be very large." This was because the Arabs were having a lot of new land cleared for cultivation and slaves would be needed for the plantations. Again the stockades at Kilwa were crowded with slaves coming in from Nyasaland.

In Zanzibar and Pemba the Arabs established themselves not only as a trading and administrative class but as a planter aristocracy whose interests were vitally concerned with the maintenance of the slave trade. Sultan Bargash was himself making £30,000 a year from "royalties" but in 1877, under British pressure, he declared that traffic by land was also illegal. But slavery still went on, for who was to deal with a slaver possessing the resources, power and wealth of Tippu Tip?

Tippu Tip's rule extended for thousands of miles west and north of Lake Tanganyika and his name was known and feared in most of East and Central Africa. So powerful was he that the great explorers, Livingstone, Cameron, Stanley and Wismann, made use of him and his intimate knowledge of the areas they explored. Through Stanley, Leopold, King of the Belgians, appointed Tip Governor of the Congo Free State in 1887. But Tippu Tip was no hero-figure; like his slaver father before him he was rapacious and cruel.

He accepted governorship of the Upper Congo because he saw that coming to terms with the Europeans was a necessary evil. It was vital for him and his fellow Arabs — and the African chiefs associated with the Arab trading system — to collect as much ivory and as many slaves as possible in as short a time as possible. Slavery was still big business in the Congo Free State and tales of the trade are told by all the travelers of the period. Between 1880 and 1890 more slaves were bought and sold in the Upper Congo than at any time before. British "interference" and the resulting difficulty of slave trading on the coast made slaves cheap and plentiful in the interior. Slaves were now essential as barter goods instead of beads and cloth. They were also used instead of paid porters and sometimes to feed the hungry raiding forces. As the Italian writer Leda Farrant observes, "Some of the most horrifying accounts of the cruelty to slaves were written during the last decade of the century when the Arabs realised that their trading paradise was coming to an end. Or perhaps it only seems more horrifying because it was better observed by an ever-increasing number of agents for European powers, and missionaries."

The year 1897 was a turning point, for Zanzibar was now a British protectorate; a decree of 1897 was more effective than all those enacted before that time. Any slave who asked for freedom was to receive it and courts could not hear the claims of slave owners. In 1909 yet another decree abolished the status of slave; there could be no such person as a slave. After this, the traditional export of slaves from the East African coast was drastically cut. Royal Navy ships were ever on the alert for slave ships and captured many of them. But unless they could be taken by surprise the slave ship captains had a terrible last resort. They carried their slaves manacled and loaded with weights so that if a naval vessel was seen approaching the slaves were dumped over the dhow's blind side and all evidence sank immediately.

The Arabs of Oman and Muscat did not give up slavery with the slow coming of civilization to East Africa. The business simply became more sophisticated, so that Negroes were now tricked into signing on for a tour of work in the Persian Gulf; their "contract" promised wages and stated that they would be returned to their homes at the end of the period. This fraud went on until the 1940s.

Dr. Paul Harrison, an American medical missionary, spent 30 years in Muscat and encountered slavery on a trip into the Bottina district of Oman, among the date plantations. Oman, he said, was "a nest of slavery." He found slaves, too, on the Pirate Coast of the Persian Gulf. "Thousands were there and with them hundreds of pearl diving boats were manned. The dark places of the earth are full of cruelty. While I was in Abu Dhabi three slaves tried to escape to Bahrein [which had abolished slavery in 1937] . . . and they were recaptured. They were beaten so severely that one of them died . . . The Baloochee slaves [from Baluchistan] were the most pathetic, they rebelled bitterly against their bonds."[4]

The African slaves taken by dhow to the pearl-fishing grounds of the Persian Gulf lived a harsh, exhausting life. Men and women were sent down with a knife and a bag in which to collect the oysters and were expected to stay below for up to four minutes at a time.

These Arab slavers and the many other merchants of Zanzibar had lived on African soil for centuries, but they had never become assimilated into the local population, which they regarded as low and inferior. Thus when Zanzibar secured independence in 1962 the entire Arab aristocracy was massacred, and the Oman dynasty which had dominated the African east coast for centuries was destroyed. This bloody revolt by the Africans of Zanzibar was the explosion of a hatred provoked by centuries of murder and oppression of Negroes by the Arabs, the vengeance cry of prisoners against foreign jailers. The Arabs exploited the native population for centuries and, as Spencer Trimingham underlines in his book *Islam in East Africa*, they did everything to maintain their exclusive power and social and religious distinction. The social discrimination of former slaves is so well established in some parts of East Africa conquered by the Arabs that even today there is a profound difference between the "slaves" and the free men "Waungwana" — those who possess a lineage from the father's side, free

---

[4]*Doctor in Arabia*, London, 1943.

from any stigma of servitude. The religious law, states Trimingham, reinforces this discrimination. The descendants of slaves, freed according to civil law, remain slaves in Moslem law and find themselves in a special position before religious tribunals, which only recognize the freedom obtained before the Moslem religious court. All this is reflected in the current life of the population. A "slave" cannot marry without first obtaining the permission of his former master and paying him a tax called "Kilemba." The religious courts can refuse to recognize the marriage, and the children are then considered illegitimate ("Nwana haram"), even though all this means nothing to the civil authorities and the marriage is perfectly legal in the law courts of the state.

Zanzibar and East Africa have an important place in the history of the Arab slave trade in modern times and, measured in terms of human misery, the region is one of the most evil in Africa.

It is worthwhile referring again to David Livingstone, who was probably the first to realize that Arab slavery caused as much misery among the black population of the African continent as had the European slave trade to America (which had just been abolished). In March, 1871, Livingstone, sick and abandoned by his men, spent four months in the town of Nyangwe near the River Lualaba, where he witnessed, powerless, an Arab attack on the local population. The slave traders arrived one market day pretending to be merchants, and attacked the Negroes, massacring hundreds of women and children and causing the death of hundreds more who were trying to escape. "It was hell," said Livingstone in a famous letter which launched a wave of British indignation. The effects of the hell he saw have yet to be finally eradicated.

IV
Saharan Slaves

The slave trade around — and across — the Sahara has probably captured public imagination and sympathy more than anywhere else, because of traditionally romantic impressions of the great desert. However, the slave trade has been anything but romantic, and the vast southern fringes where the desert meets the savanna grasslands, from Mauritania through Mali, Nigeria, Chad and the western Sudan, provided an inexhaustible supply area. In the worst days of the trade, Nigeria alone had an area of nearly 750,000 square miles (before its division into Nigeria and the new state of Niger). Here, in countless villages, the Arab slavers could work without the slightest fear of being checked by soldiers or police.

The demand for these slaves was insatiable. They were needed by the desert Arabs, the Tuareg, by the Moroccans, Algerians, Tunisians, Libyans and Egyptians. Any surplus — and the most beautiful virgins in any case — was sent to the countries of the Arabian peninsula.

The British High Commissioner wrote to London in 1901: "There is perhaps not another region in the dark continent where the hunt for slaves persists in such a terrible fashion, in such abundance and so systematically as in the British Protectorate of North Nigeria [now Niger]. Every year when the grass dries, slave traders set to work to round up the slaves. They are not prudent in their hunt, for those who are useless as slaves are killed in large numbers, the villages burned and the survivors abandoned to die of hunger in the forest."

Some slaves were kept in Nigeria, where the tsetse-fly, by destroying the cattle, caused the heavy burden of transporting merchandise to fall back on man. But a high proportion of Nigerian slaves was also transported across

Africa and sold either to Arab merchants from the north, or to the east in the Nile Valley.

One of the first Englishmen to see the slave trade operating in this region was James Richardson, sent by the Anti-Slavery Society in 1845 to investigate the trade along the Niger-Mogado route on the Atlantic coast and the Lake Chad-Tunis route. On this epic, dangerous expedition Richardson encountered a slave caravan heading for Tripoli, Libya. His diary entry for April 18, 1846, reads: "The wind is still blowing, there is a storm in the air. The sand is blowing in clouds along the road. Several women slaves have been put on camel-back in a state of extreme exhaustion. Others are driven along roughly to make them continue. Just outside Tajoura, a very young negress falls off a camel, exhausted and bleeding from the mouth. The Arabs marching alongside can make her go no further. Essnoussi [the Arab leader of the caravan] shouts 'Whip her, go on whip her!' but as no-one rushes to obey him, he jumps down from his camel, brandishing his stick . . ."

Richardson summarizes his impressions gained from his long trip:
1. Slave traffic is increasing in the Grand Desert, although it is decreasing on the Bornu route [leading to Chad].
2. Many slaves are whipped to death on the Ghat-Tripoli route and others are left exhausted, to die of hunger.
3. The Arabs and Moors submit female slaves to obscenities and most degrading tortures. Girls five years old are violated by their masters, the Tibbos, on the Bornu-Ghat route or at Fezzan.
4. Children are made to walk for more than 130 days in the Grand Desert and other regions before being sold in the markets at Tripoli.
5. Three-quarters of the slave traffic in the Grand Desert is financed by the money and goods of European merchants living in Tunis, Tripoli, Algiers and Egypt.
6. There is considerable slave traffic in the southern provinces of Algeria under French protection.
7. Slaves are Sudan and Bornu's principal trade and without slaves there would be no business.

It was the courageous Richardson who visited the Saharan slave town of Ghadames and discovered that it had a slave street and a slave sheikh or *naqib,* who told Richardson: "Be it known, O Christian! I am the Shaykh of the slaves, my name is Ahmed. I am from Timbuctoo. The people of Bambara are the finest in the world. They are brave — they fear none. Now, hear me: I know all the names of the slaves in Ghadames: I watch over all their conduct to punish them when they behave badly, to praise them when they do well. They all fear me. For my trouble I receive nothing. I am a slave myself. We have always here more than two hundred. If you wait, plenty of slaves will soon come from the Sudan!"

They came, as promised, and they continued to come. A century after Richardson, the American anthropologist James Wellard spent much time around the Sahara and investigated the slave trade. He wrote of it: "Under the efficient direction of the Arabs it involved the whole civilised world. . . .The ancient world was based on slavery, but not on African slaves. The exploitation of black labour was the contribution of the Arabs to mankind, for it was they who organised the vast traffic in human merchandise out of Africa to the Atlantic and Mediterranean ports."

Wellard stresses that "the Arabs had the advantage in the slave-trade of ferocity and religion.[1] Their attitude was extremely simple — 'Allah has created Negroes as slaves as he has made their skins black, and you can change the one as little as the other'. This was the statement made to a British Consul in 1910 by the Sheikh of the Kwaida tribe who could trace his descent from the earliest Mohammedan conquerors. The Sheikh further argued that Allah had created black men to be sold and had given to the Arabs the especial right to sell them. Neither the fact that the negroes of his old hunting ground were fast becoming Mohammedans and as such by the laws of the Koran ceased to be lawful spoil, nor the damage done to the Negro countries by continual raids, reconciled him to the new conditions. He was a true and pious Mohammedan and his alms attracted many poor to the village . . ."[2]

The decrease in Negro population was so great that Wellard estimated that the Arab merchants had brought out 5,000 slaves a year by the Fezzan route alone, losing half of them on the way. By 1900 the Lake Chad region was practically depopulated. "A few of the younger and prettier women were kept behind to entertain the Arab masters until the arrival of the next caravan. The men, the older women and the children were driven off along the road to Tripoli, to reach the next well as best they could. As a result, the route was well marked with the skeletons of adults and children, together with the grotesque carcasses of camels. . . . These avenues of bones and the stone circles marking the site of temporary mosques where the pious slave traders performed their evening rites, still mark the ancient slave-caravan routes across the Fezzan."

According to Wellard, 300,000 Africans were imported into British colonies between 1680 and 1700; the total number of Africans sent overseas as slaves from 1510–1865, when the United States abolished slavery, was at least twelve million. If we accept Dr. Livingstone's estimate that at least ten lives were lost for every one that reached the coast, the number of Africans who were captured, killed, or exported during the four and a half centuries of the slave trade is almost too great for comprehension.

---

[1] As Lord Lugard had said, "It is the most serious charge against Islam in Africa that it has encouraged and given religious sanction to slavery."
[2] James Wellard, *The Great Sahara*.

The guards on the Saharan routes never marched without their whips, which they used constantly, but the young men who had been successfully castrated and the young virgins were accorded preferential treatment; the especially beautiful virgins were carried in cages on the backs of camels.

The slave caravans which took the five trans-Saharan routes — of which the most important was Lake Chad-Bilma-Murzuk-Tripoli — were enormous, consisting of thousands of camels and thousands of slaves, for the Arab traders traveled together in a group when they could, as much for the pleasure of company as for security. Indeed, they had nothing to fear but the hostility of the tribes whose countries they crossed, and they were strong enough to fight off attacks. They were in no danger of dying of thirst for they knew the position of every well between Kano and Tripoli, and in any case, they always carried enough water for their own needs. The slaves, on foot, had no water; that is how the Arab caravaners could make them cross the desert without trouble. No captive would dare to leave the convoy unless he wanted to commit suicide. The guards had only to indicate the direction of the next well or water hole and the slaves would trudge in that direction. The only difficulty was in making them leave the wells. This they accomplished with the whip. The distances were immense; from Murzuk there was another month's journey on foot to Tripoli or Benghazi.

Moroccan imperialism, which had expanded over the centuries towards the Sudanese Savanna, and its disputes with Islamic Negro tribes of the interior, largely influenced the setting-up of Moroccan markets for slaves to be used inland and for export.

Eugene Aubin saw the slave city of Fez early this century. "In all the houses the black slaves are used as servants; negroes with heads shaved except for one frizzled ringlet and negresses whose number and clothes show at once the standing of the household. This black population was formerly imported from the Sudan via Tuat and Tafilalelt; our installation [the French] in Timbuktu abolished the trade; but today Marrakesh sends negroes from Sous, the spoil of unending inter-tribal wars in the Sahara. The slave market is held daily in the Souk el Ghzel; business seems poor but the choice products are stored away with special merchants and are sold through the medium of three well-known agents. The most popular is El Hadj Abderhaman el Kasri [who] lives near the bazaar — two rooms contain cloth and other European products; a third harbours his human merchandise — a group of very pleasant people who have just come from the South. The 'boss' is so jolly that the whole little company has an air of gaiety, and these friendly negresses are like mistresses of the house. The price for negresses varies considerably from 20 to 1,000 duros, the highest price being reached for a future concubine."[3]

[3]*Le Maroc d'Aujourdhui*, Paris, 1912.

The slave sales led to deeds of sale to be drawn up before a lawyer. An example is given by Roger le Tourneau in *Fez Avant le Protectorat:*

> Praise to God, Cherif Sidi Hachem, son of Cherif Sisi Idris Oskalli el-Hassami, has bought outright from his vendor El Hajj el-Arbi ben Abd el Chani el-Moumni, the slave whose name at the moment is El Yakout; she is coffee-coloured and quite small, has thick lips, a very flat nose and thick eye-brows. The purchaser's price has reached 30 ryals (we stress 30). The two parties made a contract and exchanged the subject and the price in ryals and owe each other nothing as is customary in these matters; they are refused any appeal after settling-up the transaction and the exchange of goods. The purchaser agreed to give up his normal rights with regard to the sale of this slave, except where she might urinate in bed, which he could not tolerate. This stipulation was brought to the cognizance of the two witnesses who made the transaction legal and binding in full possession of their faculties. The purchaser is known to the witnesses: the vendor has been made known to them as having a pointed nose, eyebrows close together and being hard of hearing. Joumadda 11 1316 23rd October, 1898."[4]

In theory, one Arab country did not condone slavery in the nineteenth century. Tunisia, in 1846, was the first Moslem state to bring in an edict of emancipation of slaves; at that time few Christian slaves remained in Tunisia, and Bey Ahmed was freeing Moslem slaves. The significance of Ahmed's decree has been discussed by Islamic jurists ever since, for while declaring that slavery was regrettable in its consequences, it stated that slavery was lawful in principle. Unfortunately, Ahmed said, in effect, masters no longer complied with the rules of good treatment of slaves and it was undesirable for Islam to have unhappy slaves seeking the protection of foreign authorities.

Despite this edict of 1846, another 44 years elapsed before effective implementation, and then only under foreign pressure. In 1875 Britain enforced a treaty with Bey Mohammad el-Sadik in which he undertook to put the earlier decree fully into effect to suppress slavery and punish any infraction. Even then, it was 1890 — by which time Tunisia was a French protectorate — before slaves were freed.

But the position was complicated and right across the Mahgreb the only hope for many slaves was that some forceful foreigner would come along and set them free. The Trappist monk Charles de Foucald, living in Algeria across the turn of the century, ransomed Negro slaves whenever he could. The first one he ransomed, in 1902, he named Joseph of the Sacred Heart and he baptized a three-year-old slave child Abd Jesu, Slave [Servant] of Jesus. Foucald was bitter about the failure of the French authorities to take energetic steps to stop slavery, for fear of offending the Tuareg slave owners and

---

[4]Published by Hautes Etudes Morocaines, 1949.

other Arab slave traders. Whenever he could scrape some francs together he would ransom slaves.

After World War Two, when the war-exhausted Powers were in no state to look into the problem of slavery, the traders of the Saharan slave belt reinvigorated a scheme that had been used effectively in the past. They engineered inter-tribal wars by promising some chief to get rid of his enemies. They said, in effect, "We will help you win your war if you will give us the prisoners; this way your enemy tribe will be weaker and can never again threaten you."

In remote parts of Africa the ruse still works, possibly with the connivance of government officials who, for reasons of their own, want to see a particular tribe weakened.

The slaves of the Tuareg, "the veiled men of the desert," are often fifth and sixth generation slaves, their ancestors having been captured in some raid a century and a half before, or bought in slave markets before the coming of French colonial administration made human trading a little more difficult. For centuries the Tuareg were not only owners but dealers, selling slaves in the northern Saharan oases to other dealers who had come from the coast or to the farmers of the oasis. Treatment of slaves varied from tribe to tribe, but generally the slave was regarded as inferior to the camel.

In the Ahaggar region a Tuareg camp generally comprises many tents inhabited by a family group which constitutes an economic cell in itself. Here slaves are owned by each family, with slaves for the men and others for the women. The ownership of slaves is personal, but the work is for all members of the family group. Such slaves are not sold and there could be 2,000 slaves for 5,000 Tuareg.

Dr. Johannes Nicolaisen of the Department of Ethnology at the University of Copenhagen lived with the Tuareg for several years and considered that in general they treated their slaves well. "They have the same life as their masters, sharing their meals, and except for rare incidences, are not subject to corporal punishment. A slave who is badly treated may change masters. He only has to cut the ear of the camel of the master he would prefer to work for, and his owner is obliged to accept his choice. Usually such a gesture is insulting for the master, and the new master may not refuse to take the slave."[5]

The gesture of cutting the ear of the camel is symbolic and represents a damage to a property. Given that the slave's master is responsible for his acts, he must pay reparation for the insult to the owner of the camel. The slave given up represents this compensation.

In a letter to the Anti-Slavery Society in 1960 Nicolaisen wrote, "I agree that slavery should be abolished. I am against any kind of slavery . . . but I

---

[5] Saetryk, *Arbog For Jysk Arkaelogisk Selskab, 1957.*

see slavery as an economic problem. You cannot abolish slavery just like that. Slavery constitutes a severe problem to be solved only by scientific studies."

But Nicolaisen would agree that the Tuareg were ruthless in some ways. They made a practice of separating slave chldren from their parents and they put some men into work that was literally killing. In the salt pits at Taodeni slaves worked all day in terrible heat with their legs in salt water; the only drinking water was also salty.

Peter Fuchs, another desert traveler in the 1950s, was also surprised by the privileged state of the Tuareg slaves. He reported that certain Tuareg had more slaves than they could keep and so freed them, but only if they were able to provide their needs by their own work.

At Atar in Mauritania, Jean Larteguy, the French writer, gained the confidence of an old interpreter, who explained to him the dirrerent castes of the society of these regions. Of slaves he said, "They are not unhappy, they are part of the family. They are born slaves and they do not want to be freed. They would not know what to do with their freedom."

One of the most recent investigators of the slave trade was Robin, Viscount Maugham, who visited Timbuktu in 1957–1958 and bought a slave — to show how easily this could be done — and freed him.[6]

Unlike the more academic travelers, Maugham was not impressed by Tuareg concern for their slaves. Their initial friendly benevolence, he found, was paper-thin. He met a beautiful slave girl, married to another slave, who had to satisfy her master's sexual wishes each night before she could go to her husband's bed. Maugham wrote, "Her huge brown eyes held the dull, empty look of a thoroughly cowed animal." This girl worked all day, pounding millet, carrying water, cooking, serving, chopping wood. Maugham noticed, too, that in contrast to the healthy plump Tuareg children the slaves' children were thin and wasted.

Lord Maugham told the House of Lords that slave boy camel-herders who lost an animal by neglect and those who were disobedient were tied up and lashed until they lost consciousness. Maugham had met a sheikh who went on pilgrimage to Mecca with six children and returned with none, because he had sold them, using them as if they were human traveler's checks. This use of slaves was commonplace throughout the worst years of the slave trade and is still practiced.

The viscount was astute enough to see that the Tuareg were waiting impatiently for the day when the French administrators would leave West Africa for good; they were even then withdrawing by stages. "Remember,"

---

[6]The story of this journey was published in *The People*, October 4 and 23, 1959. Maugham also investigated slavery in Arabia and reported in the *Sunday Post*, 1964. See also his book, *The Slaves of Timbuktu*.

he wrote in his newspaper report, "that the Tuareg regard themselves as a white race, destined to dominate and enslave the coloured peoples."

He asked two Tuareg warriors what would happen when the French finally left. One of them told him that the Tuareg would take back by force every slave the French had liberated; more than that, they would also take every Negro they could lay their hands on.

This seems to have happened. The authorities of the newly independent African states have been unable to prevent the Tuareg and other Arabs from taking slaves, despite some convictions in the courts. With the money now available for slaves the trade has been continuing. Where the slaves go to — that is, when taken outside the Saharan region — is not clear, since no adequate supervision has existed since the French withdrawal.

According to a UNESCO survey in 1965, the number of slaves — about 465,000 in all — varies from Tuareg tribe to tribe. One in seven is a slave in the Adrer, between one in six and one in three in the Ahaggar and one in three in the Air. But among the Tuareg of Gourma, south of the Niger bend, no less than three out of four are slaves.

The Moors are among the few groups left in Africa — as distinct from Arabia — who have a system of slavery little different from that of their ancestors. In their time, the French and Spanish rulers outlawed slavery, but recent studies make quite clear that it still goes on. "Slavery was outlawed under colonial rule and Mauritania's Constitution declares that all men are born free and equal before the law, but slavery remains basic in a social and economic structure largely isolated from the outside world. The juridical abandonment of the term abd [slave] and its replacement by the term hartani [freedman] for a black Moor does not hide the continued existence of slavery."[7]

Two kinds of slaves exist among the Moors — the *abd-le-tilad* who belongs to a tent like others of the nomadic household who live in the tent; and the *abd-le-tarbiyya,* who is a slave acquired by his master after infancy. There are also some descendants of slaves brought in centuries ago. The true slaves are generally black. A study carried out by UNESCO at the time of the independence of Mauritania (1960) noted that about a quarter of the Kounta people — one of the largest of Mauritania's tribes — were slaves. The warrior caste owns most slaves, although the religious caste has many. It has been alleged that a number of Moslem Black Africans from countries such as Mali and Senegal have become slaves after going to Moorish marabouts for religious teaching. A recent writer has said that, "The continued enslavement of black people by Arabs in Mauritania does not encourage the peaceful co-existence of the white and black communities in that country [and] while slavery continues there can be no real guarantee against the capture or

---

[7] A.S. Gerteiny, *Mauritania*.

purchase of new slaves. . . . The end of slavery among the Moors will not come in a hurry."[8]

In any case a big gap exists between what is supposed to be official and what happens in practise. On July 5, 1980 slavery was officially abolished in the northwest African state of Mauritania — but the practice lingers on. For generations, Blacks of Senegalese ancestry have occupied the lower ranks of Moorish society in Mauritania, even twenty years after national independence.

The traditional system of servitude stems from centuries of Arab slave trade and the 17th century conquest of Mauritania by the Moors, and its impact is still felt in many areas of this country of 2,000,000. Many of these Blacks have left their traditional slave roles in recent years, making their way into urban occupations. Most find menial jobs, though some have advanced in the army or in industry. But these freed slaves, known as "Haratine," continue to be regarded as property by a number of their Moorish masters, most of them noble families of Arab and Berber extraction. Some Haratine have apparently been returned to slavery by local authorities in the name of Islamic law.

A senior government official told the Malawi *Daily Times* (July 15, 1980) that thousands of former slaves still pay their former masters part of their crops or salary a tribute, mainly because they are convinced they will not get to heaven unless they do — a belief instilled in slave minds over the centuries by Islamic religious leaders.

In the capital city of Nouakchott, the differences between the Moors and the Blacks are startling. Many Moors live in tree-shaded houses protected by white-washed walls; most Blacks live in hovels or shabby tents. Moors generally do not perform manual labor. Black servants tend to camels, sheep and children.

The Malawi *Daily Times* correspondent in Mauritania reported:

> Moussa, 15, is the African slave of a family of Moors, Islamic people of mixed Berber and Arab blood. Moussa's father and most of his immediate ancestors were also slaves, or 'abids' as they are known in this largely feudal, Arab-dominated country. His ancestors came from the valley of the Senegal river, brought north after being captured by raiding Arab tribes. Despite this month's anti-slavery decree, Moussa still works in a poor household in sand-blown Nouakchott, faithfully obeying his master's every command. . . . Even today, according to religious sources in Nouakchott, African mothers will not take their babies with them to the fields during harvest in case they are captured as slaves by Moor tribesmen.

---

[8]Jonathan Derrick, *Africa's Slaves Today*.

V
The Agony of the Sudan

The export slave trade from the Sudan region — I use "Sudan" geographically rather than politically — is a thousand years old. As early as the late ninth century Arab slave merchants were established in Fezzan, buying from suppliers in the south. The Arab traveler Ibn Battuta, familiar with the region between 1325 – 1354, wrote that Bornu was renowned for its exports of excellent slave girls, eunuchs and dyed fabrics.[1]

At the beginning of the sixteenth century Barbary merchants were bringing war horses for the king of Bornu and exchanging them for slaves. The king was incredibly wealthy — even his dog chains were said to be of pure gold — but he paid only in slaves. He went slaving only once a year, on the horses supplied to him; so the merchants had to wait until he returned from his expedition. On occasion the slave haul was too meager to meet all the king's debts, so the Arab merchants had to wait around until the following year's hunting expedition. Passing over the many references during the next five hundred years, we come to the records left by European travelers in the nineteenth century. Two of the most observant were Major D. Denham and Captain H. Clapperton, who explored north and central Africa for much of the years 1822, 1823 and 1824. Sir H. H. Johnston has written of one of their journeys:

> After they had got past the more settled areas of Fezzan into the desert country . . . they began to see signs of the slave trade across the desert. Round most of the wells where they stopped to get water there were numbers of human bones lying about on the sands. Sometimes these remains looked as though a battle

[1] Ibn Battuta, *Travels in Asia and Africa*.

must have taken place . . . the ground being covered with whitened bones. But these were simply those of slaves who had died of thirst or hunger or been left by the caravans. The road to the Sudan indeed was lined on either side by human remains. Some were partly covered with sand. Other bodies, with the hands still pressing the head, as though to keep off some terrible headache, lay dried up. Denham counted a hundred persons' bones around one small well, with the skin still on them. The Arabs with him, however, laughed at his pain at this sight and said: 'They were only blacks.' They struck the bones with the ends of their guns, saying. 'This was a woman, this was a young man.' Denham was told that these slaves often left Bornu with very little food so that more died of hunger than tiredness or even thirst. They were made to march with heavy chains around their necks and legs.[2]

No explorer has left so much detail about slavery as the tireless and truthful German Heinrich Barth, who in 1851 watched the departure for Fezzan of a caravan of about 750 slaves; slaves were, he tells us, the main export of Bornu. In Bornu, too, Barth witnessed the appalling spectacle of 170 men in the prime of life being left to bleed to death after being wounded in a raid.

But though he saw much, Barth could not be expected to understand that during the nineteenth century the Sudan was a second main area for expansion of what can only be seen in retrospect as Arab colonialism. The clashes which took place here between Europeans and Arabs were struggles between the representatives of two groups of colonialists, each seeking the monopoly for the exploitation of the African continent. An essential difference existed between the two imperialist drives: the more economically developed Europeans struggled to free the Africans from the slave trading Arabs, knowing that the economic success of their conquest was conditioned by the presence of a native population capable, by its economic development, of paying the European administration the taxes necessary to maintain its conquest. Also, they wanted to develop purchasing power and thus change the colony to an export market reserved for the mother country. The Arabs, having nothing to bring to their African colony, were concerned only with gaining the maximum benefits from the slave trade in order to supply slave markets from Zanzibar to Brazil.

Fifty years after Europe's abolition of the slave trade, in the time of Queen Victoria and Napoleon III, slavehunting was continuing at Ouaday in the Sudanese Savanna. Sheikh Mohammad Ibn Omar El Tounssey, a participant, records that the Sultan issued "hunting permits" in a regular and legal manner, just as in Europe they were issued for hunting hare and deer.[3] The

---

[2]*Pioneers of Africa*. (Cambridge: Cambridge University Press, 1910).
[3]Sheikh Mohammad El Tounssey, ed., *Voyage au Ouaday* (Paris: 1851).

Sheikh justifies slavery in itself and the business it creates since the Negroes he hunts are pagan idolaters, men who have not yet embraced the true faith. As the Prophet Mohammad authorizes the use of force to convert men, thousands of these people were taken away and sold. El Tounssey is sorry that the pagans are not repeatedly summoned to adopt the Moslem faith before they are attacked — which does not prevent the sale being legal once they are caught, and the slaves being still considered idolaters.

Before leaving Ouaday, he bought a very strong slave who desperately wanted to escape. "As a precaution," El Tounssey says, "I kept him firmly tied with double bonds around his feet. In the night I fixed the chain, which I attached to his neck, to a stake, driven deep into the ground. Another slave, who had been in my service for a long time, leant on this chain as he slept. So guarded, my man could find no means of escaping from me. After we left Ouaday, I untied his bonds for the journey, for the night I put the chain back around his neck, and drove the stake back into the ground. . . ."

El Tounssey was impressed by the particularly thriving slave trade in Noufeh. A Moroccan merchant, wanting to show off his large fortune, came to Noufeh with a thousand slaves and more than 500 camels. But there he found merchants infinitely more rich and prosperous than he. One of them in particular, to whom he offered his goods, told him: "I have various qualities of slaves. I haven't bought a single one for a year, but if you want to buy one, I still have about ten thousand to sell. . . ."

The Sudan was "controlled" by Egypt. In Egypt as in Zanzibar slavery was part of the Moslem way of life and the government benefited very greatly from it. In the 1860s the Khedive Ismail, while paying lip service to the principle of abolishing the slave trade, was one of the largest slave owners. As for slavery in the Sudan, Ismail was well aware that all his officials were deeply involved in it; he himself had actually given state contracts to private traders authorizing them to exploit the Upper Nile. A gang of about 15,000 Arabs was bringing down at least 50,000 slaves each year. One slaver, Agad, had a government contract granting him slave trading rights over an area of 90,000 square miles, and a small private army was under his command.

In the 1860s a vast manhunt went on in the provinces of Bahr-el-Ghazel, Darfur and Kordofan. The Italian explorer Romolo Gessi estimated that between 1860 and 1873 at least 5,000 traders were operating; they had taken 4,000,000 women and children from the area, to be sold in Egypt and Turkey, and many more thousands had died. As one of General Charles Gordon's lieutenants, Gessi led an expedition against Suleiman, the son of Zobeir, ambushed him and put him to death with all his leading sheikhs. Ten thousand slaves were released — a brilliant feat. Gessi was the only European leader to understand the nature of war against the Arabs. His victory had remarkable results: for the first time in fifteen years the Western Sudan was free from the tyranny of Zobeir and his family and for a time the wholesale traffic in slaves was checked.

Yet such was the trade's resilience that Sir Samuel and Lady Baker, on their Nile expedition of 1872, found that Katiko, which they had known as a small outpost in 1864, was now a slave compound of thirty acres. At that time a healthy young girl was worth "a single elephant's tusk of the first class" or she could be bought for a new shirt or thirteen English sewing needles; these things were so much desired that parents frequently sold their children to the Arab slavers. Before Sir Samuel left, a year later, he too had reduced slavery — but it resumed soon after he turned his back.

One of the most reliable of the many foreigners who observed slavery in the Sudan was the German doctor Gustav Nachtigal, who traveled constantly in the African interior between 1869 and 1874 and left three large volumes about his experiences. For details about slaves on the march — if so dignified a word as "march" may be used — Nachtigal is incomparable. He points out that death during the slave raid itself was merely the first danger the native African had to face. Slaves were then driven like cattle into corrals; Nachtigal saw them fenced in at the camp of Abu Sekkin, ruler of Bagirmi, after raid near Kuku, central-west Sudan. The slaves so herded together in shadeless heat had little food and most were soon in poor condition and ill. Because their homeland was still fairly close and therefore presented a temptation to escape, the Arabs fastened them together by strips of rawhide. Nachtigal was angry that this was done even to people already so weak that they could barely move. Those who survived the horrors of the corral and the sorting out procedures were then put on the track for the markets. Nachtigal saw the march at close quarters and believed that for every slave who arrived three or four died on the way. This estimate squares with that of many other travelers. A German account about the Sudanese Arab slaver, Rabih, says the death rate was five-to-one while a French observer, the explorer M. Hourst, writing in 1896, considered that the sale of one captive might represent a total decline of population of ten — defenders killed in attacks on villages, women and children dying of famine, old people, children and the sick who were unable to keep up with their captors or were killed on the road because a more numerous enemy was threatening, or who died of misery. Nachtigal delivered an exhausted slave girl of her baby but both probably died soon after.

He used a guide who had bought six slaves and lost five of them on the journey; Nachtigal saved the life of the sixth, a girl who collapsed from exhaustion. With an objectivity resulting from having seen too much suffering, Nachtigal records the vicious use of the hippopotamus hide whip to keep the slaves moving. When even this could not make an exhausted slave stand up the slaver would kill him, partly from disappointment at loss of property. But always in the slaver's mind was the thought that by destroying the slave he was deterring others from any idea of feigning exhaustion to be left behind. A few slaves disappeared, usually with the help of the inhabitants of districts through which the caravan passed. When this happened the slavers would make a thorough search of all huts in nearby villages and insist that the residents swear on the Koran that they were not sheltering the missing slave and did not know where he was hiding. The use of the Holy Book for such a purpose seems deeply sad to the modern student.[4] Of course, the practice had no effect; the inhabitants of the village, often Moslem, were only too happy to acquire slaves for whom they need not pay.

Nachtigal was familiar with a spring on the road to Tibesti; the area around it was blanketed with human bones, the remnants of a slave caravan which had found the spring temporarily dry or clogged by sand and rock. About thirty years later another traveler, K. Vischer, wrote that it was always near a well that the greatest number of bones was found. He considered that they were those of slave children who had fallen by the wayside and had later dragged themselves to the well, only to find the caravan gone. This seems implausible, since the slavers, who knew the exact location of all wells, would be unlikely to abandon profitable children so close to wells that they could find their way to them.

Rudolf Anton Slatin, the Austrian soldier-adventurer who was another of Gordon's lieutenants, has left us probably the most vivid details of slavery in the Sudan in the last quarter of the nineteenth century. At the age of 21, in 1879, he became Financial Inspector of the Sennar and Gizera districts and met slavery in the course of his work.

> I found an immense collection of young women, the property of the wealthiest and most respected merchants, who had procured them and sold them for immoral purposes, at high prices. This was evidently a most lucrative trade.[5]

Slatin found that merchants sometimes pimped for their female slaves, taking a large percentage of their income.

Charles Gordon saw his mission in the Sudan as the suppression of the slave trade, but in three years of immense effort he could not suppress it. When his troops captured a party of slaves or when he bought them himself to free them, he did not know what to do with them; being so far from their homes they could not make their own way back. Gordon found, as other reformers did, that the ablest men were the slave raiders; after imprisoning them he often had to enlist them into his service. His attempts to reform the slavers were fruitless. They simply banded together against him and, when

---

[4]"All this ruthless savagery [slavery] was perpetrated in the name of religion." E.W. Bovill, in *The Golden Trade of the Moors*.
[5]*Fire and Sword in the Sudan*.

Gordon returned to England at the end of 1876 the trade was as thriving as when he had found it. The freed slaves he had collected together simply became a convenient source of supply for the Arab dealers.

Egypt had by now established herself in the heart of the Sudan and in 1877 the Khedive of Egypt, under a treaty with Britain as the ruling power, had formally banned all trade in Negroes. Offices were opened in the various provinces to check on slavery, but the dealers ignored all laws and the Africans were too ignorant to know their rights or too frightened to attempt to secure them. Back in the Sudan, Gordon appointed Slatin governor of Dara district. He served the British well for five years before he became a prisoner of the Mahdi, the "chosen one" and leader of the Dervishes, the fanatical Moslems. Earlier Slatin had announced to his own troops, all Mohammadans, that he had become converted to Islam — a deception calculated to win their support. Now it saved his life, for the Mahdi, impressed by his "conversion," made him a mulazem — a combination of servant, courtier and bodyguard. Later he became a slave and spent eight months in irons. For years he plotted to escape but remained a slave until 1895. During his long captivity he was in a unique position to see the slave trade, and his biography provides many revealing glimpses.

Mohammad Ahmed, the Mahdi, had declared a jihad or holy war against all infidels — those who did not believe in the creed of Islam and in the Mahdi as the Islamic messiah. Without any knowledge of administration or organization, the Mahdi appointed four khalifas (literally, successors) as lieutenants to shape the enormous Dervish rabble into a military and civil force. Between them, the Mahdi and the first Khalifa, Abdullah — who was later to succeed the Mahdi — exploited the Negro population of the Sudan.

The populations of towns which resisted the Mahdi's troops were treated barbarically, but few could have suffered more than those of the city of El Obeid, the most important town of western Sudan. After a long and hideous siege during which thousands of Africans died of starvation, scurvy and dysentery, El Obeid surrendered to the Dervishes. These frenzied Moslems, in a savage spree, murdered, raped and mutilated; they flogged children, servants and slaves until they revealed the hidden family valuables. The governor, Said Pasha, was tortured until he told the Mahdi the location of the state treasure and was then chopped to death with axes. Most of the population became slaves. From his vantage point, Rudolf Slatin observed the destruction of the Sudan.

> If trade in general is in a state of depression, there is one trade which has gained the great impetus from the arrival of the Mahdi, which is the slave-trade. Since the trade is prohibited in Egypt, it is developed in the provinces under the Mahdi's control. By prohibiting the export of slaves, the Mahdi acts prudently, not wanting to let his adversaries gain advantage at his expense. It

is, naturally, impossible for him to avoid the occasional export of slaves to Egypt and Arabia. A number of slaves were sent from Abyssinia and from Fachoda and also from Darfour and Nubia and offered for public sale in aid of the Public Treasury for the Khalifa's personal treasury. The transport of slaves is carried out with the same abominable and barbarous cruelty as their capture. Of the thousands of Christians of Abyssinia taken by the slaver Abou Anga, the majority are women and children who are forced, by whip, to walk the whole distance between Abyssinia and Omdurman. Snatched from their families, fed just enough to keep body and soul together, almost naked, they are driven across the country like cattle. Many die on the way, and those who do arrive in Omdurman are in such a pitiful condition that it is hard to find buyers for them and many are given away.[6]

The Khalifa recruited most of the young men to his personal guard, while the women and children were sold in the markets. Hundreds were ill and for them there were no buyers. Painfully they dragged themselves as far as the bank of the Nile to die, and as no-one undertook their burial, their bodies were simply pushed into the river. But the most terrible fate was that of the slaves who had the misfortune to be caught and sent from Darfour by the routes linking the province to Omdurman. Slatin says, "They were driven on, day and night, without water, and it is impossible to describe the cruel means the slavers used to bring their victims to their destination. When they could go no further, their ears were cut off to be shown to the owners [the entrepreneur dealers] on arrival, as proof that their merchandise had died en route."

Slatin provides one of the best eye-witness descriptions of a Sudanese slave market:

> Round the walls of the house numbers of women and girls stand or sit. They vary from the decrepit and aged half-clad slaves of the working class to the gaily-decked concubine; and as the trade is looked upon as a perfectly natural and lawful business, those put up for sale are carefully examined from head to foot, without the least restriction, just as if they were animals. The mouth is opened to see if the teeth are in good condition. The upper part of the body and the back are laid bare and the arms are carefully looked at. They are then told to take a few steps backward or forward in order that their movements and gait may be examined. A series of questions are put to them to test their knowledge of Arabic. In fact, they have to submit to any examination the intending purchaser may wish to make.
>
> Concubines . . . vary considerably in price. . . . Only occasionally can one see by the expression of a woman or girl that she feels the close scrutiny; possibly her position with her former master was rather that of a servant than a slave or she may have been looked upon almost as a member of the family and may have been brought to this unhappy position . . . through some hateful inhumanity on the part of her former master. When the intending purchaser

[6]Ibid.

has completed his scrutiny he then refers to the dealer, asks him what he has paid for her or if he has any better wares for sale. He will probably complain that her face is not pretty enough, that her body is not sufficiently developed and so on, with the object of reducing the price. . . . On the other hand, the owner will do his utmost to show up her good qualities, charms etc. . . . Among the various "secret defects" which oblige the owner to reduce the price are snoring, bad qualities of character, such as thieving . . . but when at last the sale has been finally arranged, the paper is drawn out and signed, the money paid, and the slave becomes the property of her new master.[7]

On any day in the Omdurman *souk er rekik* (slave market), about fifty or sixty women and thirty or so men would be offered for sale. Their thin bodies were rubbed with oil to give them a sleek appearance, and the owners recited aloud the pedigrees of their victims in the manner of auctioneers at a cattle market. Women slaves were more in demand than men and a black skin was preferred to copper-colored. An Austrian priest, Father Joseph Phwalder, noticed that Arab women owners were more cruel to their retainers than men; it was common to see a woman gash a disobedient slave with a knife and order salt to be poured into the wound.

In the market at Omdurman, prices — for women and children, since the men were reserved for the Khalifa — were lower if the slaves could not speak Arabic, but in 1885-87 average prices were £20 for an old slave still capable of working, £35-50 for a middle-aged woman, £50 – 75 for an 8 – 11 year old girl, according to her beauty.

In Bornu, as elsewhere, the *sedasi* — a boy who measured six spans from his ankle to the tip of his ears — was a particularly valuable property. The *sedasi* — the word comes from the Arabic — were aged usually from twelve to fifteen and their price was a reliable guide to slave prices generally. *Sedasi* are mentioned in much of the popular poetry and songs of the Sudan. Bornu also had a brisk trade in boys and girls of the five-span group (ten to thirteen years). Seven-span boys (fifteen to twenty), while they brought good prices, were more difficult to train and more likely to run away. Several European observers, notably Nachtigal, noted that deaf-and-dumb slave girls were much sought after as servants for the magnates of the Moslem world in Europe, Asia and Africa. Dwarfs, a favorite plaything for Moslem princes, were only a little less costly than eunuchs. We have the evidence of F.S. Arnot that Arab slavers threw away children too small to walk; Arnot collected a small family of them.[8]

In addition to the enormous demand for slaves for export to the Moslem north, there were gigantic needs to be satisfied in the Sudan itself, where

[7]Ibid.
[8]*Garenganze, Seven Years' Pioneer Mission Work in Central Africa*, London, 1889.

many a chief owned thousands of slaves. Consequently the raiding of pagan — that is, non-Moslem — tribes in the hills and forests became a major occupation of Moslems throughout the whole length of western Sudan.

Rahman Zobeir, father of the slaver executed by Gessi and head of the family slaving business, had carved for himself an immense territory in southern Sudan. Zobeir owned a strong private army in Bahr-el-Ghazel and in 1874 he offered to combine with the Egyptians in an attack on the rebellious tribes of the Darfur region. As it happened, Zobeir was so powerful he went into battle without the Egyptians; he defeated the tribesmen, killed the Sultan of Darfur and then controlled an area far larger than France. It was an impressive display of the slavers' strength and it showed the difficulty of overcoming their slavery operations.

Zobeir's political influence is illustrated by the English viceroy of Egypt, Lord Cromer, in his memoirs published in 1906. Describing Zobeir as the supreme slave merchant in the Sudan, he reports the long negotiations between the English Agency at Cairo and the English Government, to obtain the Government's agreement to name Zobeir as Governor of the Sudan and successor to General Gordon and to award him a high distinction. It had, in fact, been acknowledged in Cairo and in Khartoum that only Zobeir, a man of "exceptional qualities," could resist the Mahdi and save Gordon, besieged in Khartoum. The proposal was rejected for fear of the reaction of English public opinion and the British Anti-Slavery Society. Nevertheless, Prime Minister Gladstone had, at one time, agreed to use the services of the slave merchant and to "give" him Sudan as a last means of saving Gordon's life and the standing of the Egyptian Government, which was Gordon's responsibility in Khartoum.

Long after Gordon's time Khartoum depended on the slave trade. Any Arab adventurer could set up as a trader if willing to borrow money at up to eighty per cent interest. On a normal expedition a slaver would sail south from Khartoum in December with about 250 armed men and form an alliance with a native chieftain. Then the Khartoum slavers and the tribesmen would attack some sleeping village, firing the huts just before dawn and shooting into the flames. The slavers chiefly wanted the women, who were secured by placing a heavy forked pole known as a sheba on their shoulders. The head was locked in by a crossbar, the hands were tied to the pole in front, and the children were bound to their mothers by a chain passed round their necks. Everything the village contained would be looted.

The closest point of sale for the captives was northern Sudan, whose Arab population strongly disliked menial labor, especially agricultural labor. In this society, as in much of the Arab world, a man achieved higher status by cutting down on the amount of his menial work, even on his own land. Also, to work for someone else was socially humiliating. Many centuries before,

these northern Sudanese began to bring in by force other peoples to do all the menial and socially undesirable work. The supply was plentiful, and as Peter F.M. McLoughlin has shown,[9] there were several sources:
1. Sudanic people of the Nuba Mountains.
2. Sudanic people of the western Sudan mountains.
3. Sudanic peoples in the central-eastern Sudan near the Ethiopian border.
4. Nilotic, Nilo-Hamitic, Negroid and other southern Sudan peoples.
5. Abyssinia (later Ethiopia).
6. Belgian Congo, French Equatorial Africa, Kenya, Uganda, (along the White Nile and Bahr el ·'Arab; through Bahr-el-Ghazel province and over several main routes which entered north-western Sudan).
7. The pilgrimage from West Africa to Mecca.

McLoughlin also lists the main slave trading groups:
1. Nomads (a) Central and western Sudan Arab nomads
   (b) Hadenowa peoples in eastern Sudan.
2. Moslem agriculturalists along the Nile north of Khartoum to the Egyptian border.
3. Moslem agriculturalists along the White and Blue Niles south of Khartoum.
4. Urban Khartoum and Omdurman.
5. Outside Sudan: (a) Slaves shipped to Arabia (pilgrimage was also used for this purpose) (b) extended North Africa markets — Egypt, Tripoli, Palestine (c) West Africa; slaves captured in Kordofan, Darfur and south of the Bahr el 'Arab would be passed to Northern Nigeria, Niger, Mali and Mauritania.

It should be noted that several Moslem societies lived in West Africa, as in Mauritania, for instance, long a profitable market for the slavers. In Mauritania it was said that a slave from the Sudan used to be bought with a bar of salt the length of his foot, but by the nineteenth century a camel load of salt was necessary to buy a slave, male or female, and even then something might be owing. Salt exporters from Mauritania went to the Sudan and returned with slaves, some of whom were used to pay debts contracted at the time of the traders' departure, some sold to neighboring people. Slaves figure largely in literature of the arms trade. In Liberia, for instance, the value of a slave boy was fifteen kegs of gunpowder while a girl would bring ten kegs.

Virtually all slave routes involve the Sudan, for geographical, historical, political and religious reasons. Geographically, the Sudanese coast is the closest to that of Saudi Arabia and the two major ports — Port Sudan and

---

[9]In a long essay, "Economic Development and the Heritage of Slavery in the Sudan Republic," reprinted from *Africa,* October, 1962, by the International African Institute. This essay is an impressive piece of detailed research.

Suakin — are opposite the Arabian port of Lith and fairly close to the markets of Jedda, Mecca and Taif. From Suakin the slave traders' small boats left also for the south, for Jezzan and for the coast of Yemen. Other traffic left also from the coast of Somalia and Kenya, but in smaller numbers because of the fairly long voyage and because of the control which the Ethiopian authorities imposed on all traffic to their territory. For the slave caravans coming from western Sudan (the French region), Mali, the Central African republic, North Nigeria, Chad, the south Sahara, the route in the Nile area of the Sudan was traditionally not only the shortest but the most certain in slave supply.

For centuries the main route followed by the slavers was that which united occidental Africa with oriental Africa, north of the high Ethiopian plateaux. Each water point, each plantation of palm trees, each oasis and village and every route was known. Many had been established by the slavers; they were often the only resting places for the caravans, as all around were deserts. In this region for generations the commercial, social, and political threads of life were united to make of the Sudan a large Arab slave market.

At times the great slave owners held more slaves than they could possibly use or sell, so that a healthy man could be bought for practically nothing. Yet the slavers continued to organize slave hunts, to encourage gifts of slaves and to compel the payment of slave debts. The "principle" behind this obsession with slave collection appears to have been that without an adequate supply of slaves the great man could not reward his followers or pay his own debts. Two modern scholars on Moslem slavery, Allan Fisher and Humphrey Fisher, suggest that the stockpiling of slaves "may be plausibly interpreted as indicating that the principle enunciated by Adam Smith in his analysis of the economics of slavery, 'the pride of man makes him love to domineer' could be a main factor".[10]

The Sudan slavers, operating in a vast area of varied climate and terrain, ran all kinds of commercial risks and in conversations with European travelers, and occasionally in their own records, they show that they were deeply worried about the hazards they ran. One risk was smallpox, which caused a slave caravan, or any other group of travelers, to be shunned by everybody. Many a slaver, discovering the dread disease in his caravan, preferred to cut his losses and abandon the slaves rather than risk catching the disease himself.

Barth knew as a friend Al-Haj Bashir, ruler of Bornu in 1851, who set off on holy pilgrimage with a party of slaves he proposed to sell along the way to cover his expenses. One night, in the mountains between Bornu and Fezzan, forty of the slaves died of cold. Bashir told Barth that he had learnt a bitter lesson — never to travel with slaves for sale, for the financial risk could

[10]*Slavery and Moslem Society in Africa.*

be ruinous. Barth could not make him see that the slaves had lost more than money. Other travelers found groups of slaves (or their bones) who had died of cold.

In strict economic terms, slave trading was indeed a gamble — as so many dealers complained. But they took no precautions to see that their property had every chance of survival in good condition. If slave owners could be so brutally negligent, how much more so were the slave drivers, who contracted only to deliver the survivors of a caravan at a certain market. James Richardson once encountered Tuareg slave drivers moving a caravan from Ghat in the Tibesti Mountains to Ghadames, south of Tripoli; peering into the distance he made out two old men struggling after the snaking caravan. On closer examination he discovered that the old men were two small children crawling. They did not survive, and the Arabs knew that they wouldn't.

In the early 1900s one of the most infamous slave raiders, Ibrahim Wad Mahoud, practically depopulated some regions. The Bornu tribes were particularly hard hit and an official British report of 1903 from the Blue Nile Province stated that "It is pitiable . . . the devastation wrought by Ibrahim Wad Mahoud. In the sphere in which he raided there are no children left, the proportion of adults is about seven men to one woman, and the villages are devoid of sheep, goats, poultry and cattle." He was caught and hanged the following year.

When the English and Egyptians set up a condominium in 1899, the British more actively restricted the Sudanese trade. Some fights against slavers were big enough military actions to warrant the issuance of a bar to the Khedive's Sudan Medal.

Despite the successes, the area was too vast for the small British forces to do more than inconvenience the slavers until the defeat of the Mahdist movement in 1908 made it difficult for the slavers to operate.

Even after the Mahdist period the problems were immense. The official British Report on Egypt for 1920 refers to one great difficulty which occurred when Darfur came under British administration from Khartoum. As a result of the death of Ali Dinar, the slave ruler of Darfur

> . . . a great number of slaves, principally women, were cast adrift, and in the confusion which ensued before the country began to settle down under our administration there was a general scramble for the possession of these masterless slaves . . . when bands of Arabs went across the border to try to get a portion of the loot.

The British administered the northern Arab regions and the southern Negro regions separately. The well-selected British experts, through hard work and skill, turned parts of the vast country — more than 2,500,000 square miles — into a garden, producing millions of bales of cotton and corn and supporting a population of nearly 13,000,000. The Sudanese Arab politicians have blamed this British policy of keeping the north and south separate for all that followed; they claimed that the British deliberately closed the south to the Arabs and this, they say, created the separatist drive which followed independence. In fact, the British were respecting a separatism that was naturally in existence, for the southern natives remembered all too vividly the Arab slave raids and did not trust the Arabs enough to mix with them. The British knew from experience that the Arabs and Africans simply could not mingle; the Arabs invariably exploited the blacks. In this respect the report of a former senior colonial administrator of the French Sudan on the introduction of large-scale cultivation of groundnuts makes significant reading. Noting that the nuts were to be processed by an oil-extracting factory on the spot, the administrator wrote:

> The Moslem chieftains understood very well what they could get out of the factory, out of this threat of 6,000 tons [the quota called for] which hung over the countryside. The more the White man called for "produce" — cotton, millet, groundnuts — the more they accused the peasants of laziness. They transformed them into serfs, they brought them to the seigniorial fields, they kept them surrounded by overseers, they armoured themselves by saying they were acting on behalf of the French. Upon the ruin of the tribal holdings they set up large estates. . . . The profit went to the chieftain and his numerous overseers. Nothing was left to pay the peasants, who had been turned into serfs and dispossessed of their soil . . . the fields were cultivated by forced labour.[11]

In the 1950s, with colonialism dying in most parts of the world, the British prepared to leave Sudan and with the Egyptians agreed on a system of government, without consulting the Africans of the south. The Africans, nevertheless, made their point of view clear — they could accept union with the north and the Arabs if it was a federal union. That is, they wanted a form of democratic government. At that time about 58 per cent of the overall population were Africans, though at least half were bush dwellers with no interest in national politics.

Despite their agreement with the British, the Egyptians began a campaign not to let this flourishing region slip from their grasp. In 1952 Colonel Naguib, a Sudanese Arab himself, pulled off a coup when he and Colonel Nasser secured agreement to the speedy election of a Sudanese Legislative Assembly, to be followed three years later by a referendum. Naguib and Nasser believed they could fix the referendum in favor of a union with Egypt. But when Naguib arrived in Khartoum as Egypt's principal delegate to the

---

[11] Robert Lelavignette. *Les Paysans Noirs*. Paris, 1946.

first Sudanese parliament, anti–Egyptian tribesmen attacked the palace where he was staying. It was an indication of the apprehension the Sudanese were feeling. Sensing what was to come, black soldiers of the Sudanese army mutinied against the Arab officers who were replacing the British. The Arabs put down the mutiny savagely and hundreds of black soldiers took to the bush.

On independence in 1956 Moslem Arabs were soon in control in Khartoum; Arabic was proclaimed the official language, Islam became the "right" religion and all administration, for north and south, passed into Arab hands. The "southern slaves" — as the Arabs called the Africans — were soon suffering under racial discrimination and economic exploitation. A new kind of slavery was beginning.

The Sudanese Arab leaders were thinking imperialistically, as Abu Ibrahim Mohammed expressed in the *Egyptian Journal* of April 10, 1963: "It would be desirable for the union of Sudan and Egypt to cover territory from Eritrea to Nigeria to allow the creation of an African Islamic empire."

The southern Sudan provinces of Upper Nile, Equatoria and Bahr-el-Ghazel held about 3,000,000 people, against a possible 9,000,000 in the six northern Arab provinces. The quarter-million Christian Negroes of the south, the better-educated ruling class, expected to retain part of the provincial autonomy they had held under the British, but the Arabs denied them any authority. The declaration sent on January 10, 1962, by the Committee of National Liberation of South Sudan to the Secretary of the United Nations was entitled: "Arab Colonialisation and Oppression in South Sudan." It alleged that the state of emergency of the Khartoum Government — under which entry into South Sudan was forbidden to all foreigners and especially to non-Sudanese blacks — was intended to make impossible any witnessing of what was happening there, and to keep the South as "a human zoo."

The Congolese (Brazzaville) newspaper *The African Week* on March 15, 1962, published a report on the "Arab war" in the Sudan.

> The uniqueness of the Sudanese Africans is to be in exile in their own country. One meets Sudanese in all corners of Africa, and their story is always the same: it is a story of genocide, of religious persecution and racial discrimination. A century after the abolition of slavery, the Arabs have established new colonialism and a new slave trade — their own dominion over the blacks of the South of the country. This vast country was once one of the richest sources of slavery in the continent. During their colonisation of Sudan, the English put an end to this disgraceful practice, and shocked the Arab inhabitants of the North by making them equal to the blacks of the South. But the Arabs never, in fact, accepted the blacks as their equals and on independence they established the old situation. . . . Arabs have been given the right to take black women as wives and concubines but severe prison sentences are imposed on blacks who allegedly insult Arab women. Everything which is happening makes it impos-

sible to believe that it concerns equal citizens of the same country. Many refugees speak of their disappointments. They had hoped for much from their independence but they quickly realised that they had overcome the Anglo-Egyptian domination merely to fall under the domination of the Arabs, Arabs from their own country, and a situation much worse than anything which they had had in the past. . . .

A Swiss journalist, Walter Staehnelin, was also worried about the resurgence of slavery and wrote in the *Basler Nachrichten,* in August, 1962, that hundreds of Sudanese blacks were being transferrred to the north of their country to become slaves there or to be sent to Saudi Arabia, the Yemen and other oil "sheikhats."

The president of the National Sudanese Union of the "Forbidden Zone," Joseph Odubo, a member of parliament before independence, was arrested as an agitator and put up for sale for £800, but escaped to Uganda. From here he announced that the Arab takeover was accompanied by attacks on villages, assaults of "incredible cruelty" against the civilian population and the destruction of all local economic and cultural issues so that the Arabs could more easily uproot the Sudanese Africans and settle in the south themselves. Odubo said, "The Arabs have executed many hundreds of Africans, they have burned 12,000 homes, and confiscated cattle to the value of £500,000. They have raped our women, closed all schools, hospitals, orphanages, maternity hospitals, leper colonies and missions."

African students in London sent a petition to the Sudanese president Ibrahim Abboud when he made a state visit to Britain in May, 1964, denouncing "the racialist and misguided religious ideology of the Arabs who dominate the country politically and economically. . . . It is a struggle for survival in the face of ruthless efforts to assimilate them [the Africans] or wipe them out. . . . We denounce the savage campaign of terror, killing and repression in the Southern Sudan. . . ."

The Africans' resentment developed into sporadic acts of revolt. The Khartoum mutineers hiding in the bush occasionally sniped an Arab officer or fired on a Nile steamer and this produced savage reprisals. For ten years the Arabs warred against the Negroes with a ferocity equaled only by that of the Iraqis against the Kurds. But the rebels, now organized as the Anya Nya movement (named for a deadly snake) held the bush. Arab reprisals for alleged guerrilla activity were violent. In July, 1965, for instance, at Juba, Equatoria, an army sergeant was murdered. The Arab troops hunted down the population like wild beasts; missionaries said that on the night of July 8 about 1,500 Negroes were killed. A few days later about a hundred people who had come to a wedding in Wau, Bahr-el-Ghazel, were slaughtered. In January, 1967, in the Torit region of Equatoria, government troops burned down six villages and killed 400 of their inhabitants. Film director

Dino de Laurentiis filmed a scene of Sudanese Army brutality, as did British television.

All Christian schools and missions were closed down and many churches destroyed. Foreign missionaries were expelled and African Christian clergy either fled or waited to be killed. Out of all this confusion a few statistics emerged. The *Journal de Genève,* on September 9, 1967, estimated that half a million Africans had been killed. The United Nations thought that 115,000 refugees had gone to neighboring countries, a figure since known to be greatly conservative; ultimately it was about one million. Probably another half a million had taken to the Sudanese bush. To cut off the Africans' flight the Arab army "cleared a corridor" forty miles wide along the southern Sudan frontier, a process which involved burning down hundreds more villages and killing their inhabitants. Many young Negro boys and girls were taken as slaves; many were sent to Arab homes in the north — where they remain — or were sold to the slave dealers who had followed the troops.

The Italian journalist Fabrizio Dongo, in a report sent from Khartoum to many Italian newspapers in 1966, said that "the Arabs continue in the Sudan what could be called their national sport, hunting slaves, and the bondage of Negro Sudanese who are guilty not only of having a black skin but also of not being Moslems."

The major Italian paper *Il Corriere della Sera* reported in its editorial of July 30, 1966, under the title of "Genocide in Sudan," that during the Mahdist regime, at the end of the nineteenth century, the population of the Sudan decreased by four-fifths because of the Arab slave trade — from 8 million the population decreased to 1,800,000. It expressed the desire that the new Government of Seddik el Mahadi would put an end to the genocide of the blacks. Odubo, the head of the Sudanese National Liberation Movement, was skeptical. "In the past, the Arabs at least only sold us, now they only want to kill us."

Under cover of independence and newly acquired sovereignty, the Arab slaver, inspired by oilwealth and helped by the weakness of the new administrations of African countries freed from the yoke of colonialism, began to revive the trade. In the Sudan, all conditions necessary for the trade are united: racial hatred of the Arab for the black, the spite of the Moslem for the non-Moslem, fortunes made in the hunt for man, and the renewal of Arab colonization in Africa.

The National Sudanese Union, on March 27, 1967, published a new ". . .call for liberation. We fear that the Arabs will . . . send the blacks to wander in the desert. . . . If this imminent catastrophe is not stopped, the tribes of the South Sudan, who are among the most intelligent and industrious of the continent, will be wiped out. . . . All the ex-colonies of the African continent who have gained independence, have acquired the right to decide their own destiny, but we in Southern Sudan have seen ourselves refused this right. Portugal, France and Britain have been accused of acts of repression in their colonies — shootings, hangings, etc. This is exactly what the Arabs are doing in Sudan. How is it possible to condemn the whites who committed atrocities against the African blacks, and not the Sudanese Arabs who commit these same atrocities against defenceless blacks in Southern Sudan? As long as certain races believe in their superiority over the black race, as do the Arabs of Northern Sudan, we think that the unity of the continent between black and Arab races from Northern Africa will not take place.''

To make the crushing of the Africans complete the Arabs ruled that only Arabic could be taught in the primary schools — high schools were barred to Africans and reserved for children of the Sudanese Arabs who were moved in to administer and control the south. Despite the ban on foreign journalists and other visitors, news of the enslavement of the Sudanese Africans did reach the outside world.

Changes of governments have given the Sudanese Africans no relief. General Abboud's military government, which had come to power through a coup in 1958, was overthrown in 1964 by a civilian rising. Under successive civilian governments the problem of southern Sudan deteriorated still further. In May, 1969 a group of army officers and left-wing civilians under General Numeiri came to power in a bloody coup. The new regime announced an amnesty for African ''rebels'' willing to co-operate but with experience of previous betrayals the Anya Nya movement continued to fight. To surrender, they said, would mean offering themselves as slaves — and Sudanese Africans had seen enough slavery. Nevertheless, in southern Sudan, the Africans *are* slaves.

Commenting on slavery in the Sudan, Alan Moorehead has said that ''Probably nothing more monstrous or cruel than this traffic has happened in history.'' The judgment does not seem extravagant.

VI
Saudi Arabia: Slavery As Part of a Lifestyle

The Arabian Peninsula, that vast area stretching from the border of Russia to the Persian Gulf and the Red Sea and westward to the Mediterranean, was always a market for slaves. Over the centuries many millions of white and black people of scores of races have disappeared into its mysterious towns and desert wastes. Over these centuries millions of Arabians — to use a general term — were ready to buy slaves to increase their status, reduce their own work and heighten their pleasures. A region of countless kings, princes, sheikhs and sultans, Arabia had an insatiable appetite for human flesh; a use could be found for it, regardless of its condition. A pretty girl was a concubine, a young boy a homosexual prostitute, a middle-aged woman a cook or maid, an elderly man a gardener. Nobody was too old to sit at a door and open it when his master wished to pass through it, nobody so weak that at least a few months' work could not be squeezed out of him before he died.

Yet, as a "grand" slaver, Arabia succeeded Tunis, Tripoli, Algiers, Cairo, the southern states of the United States and Brazil. It was not that fewer slaves were sold in Arabia but that the sales were less visible. The focus of attention finally fixed on Arabia because, at a time when the trade was dying in most parts of the world, it was gaining new life in Arabia. This was not generally admitted. It was frequently denied and even more frequently an accusation of slavery produced the challenge, "Prove it!" Proof has been forthcoming from many sources, not least from Arabic ones. For instance, slavery was protected by law in Saudi Arabia and Yemen until 1962, implicit admission of its existence.

It is hardly necessary to explore the history of slavery in Saudi Arabia as we did in the Sudan; the larger, deeper history is well known and recorded. Saudi Arabia and her neighbors provide a study of modern slavery under entirely new conditions.

These countries came late to the twentieth century. Foreign diplomats sent to the Persian Gulf or south Arabia in the 1930s felt, with reason, that they had been pitche- backwards in time, that they were serving in frontier territories among "natives" and "savages." One such diplomat in that decade was Harold Ingrams, who was British Resident Adviser in the Hadhramaut states — now Yemen. Ingrams' work was important here and elsewhere in Arabia, but it is his wife, Doreen, who has left us the more colorful details of the ways of life in south Arabia in *A Time in Arabia*. She writes of the Ja'adi tribe, notorious as kidnappers and slavers in the 1930s. At local festivals in honor of various holy men they sold men for about £45, and women, priced at £60. Mrs. Ingrams knew that Ja'adi men often visited Hyderabad, India, to get hold of Moslem boys under the pretext of giving them a good Moslem religious education in the lands of the prophet Mohammad. They sold the boys as slaves at the first opportunity.

She tells of a Ja'adi who married a Hindu girl and at once sold her and her son to his brother in payment of a debt. The brother sold them to another tribesman. The woman, driven to desperation, sought refuge with Harold and Doreen Ingrams, who contacted her family in India and shipped her back to them, together with her son and another Indian slave boy the Ingrams had rescued.

Sometimes masters imposed bizarre conditions. Mrs. Ingrams records the case of a freed male slave who had married a slave woman — but her master had consented to the marriage only on condition that half her children belonged to him. The former slave and his wife had two sons and wanted to keep both; so the master viciously attacked her to make her give up one son. Mrs. Ingrams arranged for the wife to be freed and the master then had no power over her.

In Mrs. Ingrams' time in south Arabia slaves were a major part of the community, a class in themselves. Even those who had been freed were still called slaves. A convention had been held in Geneva in 1926 and an International Bureau of Slavery set up but, not unnaturally, it had not even been heard of in Saudi Arabia and nothing could have come of it in any case.

One of the most tireless of slavery researchers was Eldon Rutter who travelled extensively in Arabia in the 1920s and 1930s. Interested in the paradox that the Arab race had done so much for the advancement of mankind yet could practise and prolong slavery, he believed that the reasons lay in the extreme insularity of the Arabs and the fact that "slavery itself is congenial to the Arab character." This, in turn, was due to the Arab's desire to have as many dependants about him as possible. "He likes to see them sitting about his doorway at all hours of the day and night, awaiting his commands."[1]

Rutter is one of the few serious students of the Arabs who explains why they prefer to buy their servants outright rather than hire them. Unlike the paid servant, the "slave cannot go away at his own will." The most he could do was to beg his master to be so good and kind as to sell him to somebody else.

It is Rutter, too, who makes one of the most significant points about the Arab's use of women. In Mohammedan marriages a dowry must be paid by the bridgegroom. If a man is dissatisfied with a wife he can divorce her at once but he cannot regain possession of her dowry. However, a slave-concubine who proves unsatisfactory can be promptly sold and the man is unlikely to lose financially on the deal. Undeniably, many slaves in Saudi Arabia have lived a contented life. For this very reason Rutter condemns it. "Let there be no contented slaves. A social system which rears men to be so ignorant and devoid of spirit that they are contented to be bondsmen, and which rears others so insensitive that they are contented to own, to buy and to sell their fellow-men like cattle, carries its own condemnation. . . ."

Contentment is a relative word and it could hardly be applied in any degree to some slave women. For instance, over the centuries Mecca has been full of students who settle in the city for years to study theology. Arabs of the town were quick to discover that these students would pay for the right to cohabit with a slave woman, and "marriages" were arranged. Sometimes a genuine affection would develop but the student was almost invariably too poor to buy his woman's freedom. He found, too, that any child born to him and his "wife", became the property of the woman's owner.

Sir George Macmunn, a contemporary of Rutter, understood very well the desire Arab men felt for a Negro woman. "She is very popular as a concubine in the summer for her black skin keeps surprisingly cool while that of an Arab does not. When during the Great War the British forces came to the Tigris the word went round among the Arabs that now the British had come all the slaves would be freed. The Arabs petitioned the British not to free the women "because of the advantages of coal-black skin." Macmunn saw no possibility of the trade diminishing. "Since men and women are bought and sold as slaves the slave womb is kept busy by both slaves and Arab masters. Ten of thousands have been born slaves of slave mothers in Arabia. . . .[2]

A particularly inhuman aspect of Arabian slavery was pointed out by G.E. de Jong in 1934. "It is little known that in Arabia, Mecca and the Yemen corps of slave men and women are maintained and bred like cattle in order

---

[1] In a lecture to the Anti-Slavery Society, March 15, 1933
[2] *Slavery Through the Ages*. (London: Nicholson and Watson), 1938.

that their children may swell the slave markets."[3] He cited Eldon Rutter in support of his statement.

The tireless British continued to press for abolition in Arabia. As a token of good will, King Ibn Saud abolished the customs duty formerly levied on the import of slaves. In 1927 he told the importunate British legation at Jedda that all slaves who claimed their freedom could have it. Not surprisingly, between 1930 and 1935 only 150 slaves claimed this right. Slave owners made it clear to their slaves that claiming freedom was dangerous.

In 1934 the British induced the Imam of the Yemen to prohibit the entry of slaves coming from Africa. This led to similar agreements with the sultans and sheiks in the East Aden protectorate and the Persian Gulf, including the Sheikh of Kuwait who declared all traffic in slaves to be illegal. As always, these edicts were no more than inconveniences for the slavers.

Until 1936 British consulates had the right to set free any slave who took refuge there. Traditionally, the slave grasped the pole from which flew the Union Jack; this act unfailingly gave him all the formidable protection of the British Crown. But on October 3, 1936, the British renounced this right, and after that date fugitive slaves seeking asylum were returned to their masters. This betrayal profoundly changed the attitude of many insignificant people towards the British. Even the people most likely to benefit from the change of policy — the slave owners — felt some contempt for the British. Of course, the new policy directly followed the promulgation of the Saudian law of slavery on October 2, 1936 — a law which purported to end slavery but did not do so. Politically legitimate, the British decision to give up the right to set slaves free was, in human terms, premature by three decades.

The war of 1939 – 45 created further inconveniences, but it also removed international interference and observation and throughout the Arabian peninsula the trade flourished.[4] After the war slavery came back into the news and in 1946, the Syrian press showed that an open state of slavery existed in the country, which had only just achieved independence. Under the title "The Slave Trade in the Alaouite Area of Syria" the newspaper *Al Insha* wrote on September 24, 1946, that no measure had been taken by the Government to put an end to this slavery, organized by a well-known group of merchants from Latakia.

A year later, in December 1947, another Syrian publication, *Al Toumaidoun al Islami*, revealed that Syrian girls were "sold like cattle" and that

---

[3] Article in the *Moslem World*, April 1934.
[4] It is interesting to note that during World War II the United States and Great Britain gave Saudi Arabia — that is, the king — enormous subsidies. The U.S. contributed $17,500,000 worth of Lend-Lease, although Saudi Arabia was neutral and served as a sanctuary for Nazis and war criminals. The Americans also lent King Ibn Saud several million ounces of silver, none of which was returned. In 1946 the U.S. Export-Import Bank granted him a loan of $10,000,000, and none of this money was returned. Britain provided the king with sovereigns, silver riyals and sterling credits which overall amounted to more than the U.S. sudsidy.

enormous fortunes were made by merchants and intermediaries in the slave trade. After the official prohibition of prostitution in Syria, it was calculated that in one year 3,000 young girls had been bought to be sent to secret brothels in the country.

Conditions had not changed much by 1954, as the *Syrian Press Bulletins* of October 16 and 19 showed:

> The paper *Alef Baa* [Damascus] of 16 October is devoting its headline to exposing the game of certain Saudi nationals who marry young Syrian girls to do business with them in Saudi Arabia. For some time, says the paper, it has been noticed that the marriages between young Syrian girls and Saudi Arabians who gave lavish presents to their parents, pretending to be princes of royal blood or high-ranking in their country, have multiplied. These young wives soon write of their lamentable situation; having been played with by their husbands, who turn out to be ordinary workers, who merely married these young Syrians in order to gain favour with princes and rich Saudis. Following complaints to the Government, secret agents were sent on mission to Saudi Arabia during the time of pilgrimage, to discover the true situation of these young Syrian wives. Their reports confirmed the facts, and the Syrian Government reported the situation to the Embassy of Saudi Arabia. It was agreed that no marriage between Syrians and Saudis would take place without an official report giving details of the financial state and social position of the man in question. The parents of the young girls would thus have all necessary information and would therefore be directly responsible for the situation of their daughters.

In September 1955, the French journalist, Raymond Loir, wrote in the *Echo d'Alger*:

> ". . . . In a country as developed as Syria, I saw many dwellings of old black slaves. They were part of the family, and the young men and young girls whom they had brought up, respected them almost as much as their parents. During the Turkish period, it was the custom for the well-off Syrian families to buy slaves. This custom no longer exists. Nevertheless in the Alaouite mountains, poor parents hire out their children for five or ten years. It is a new form of slavery, and the Syrian Government never thought to forbid this practice. I remember that at the end of the French mandate in Syria, the Alaouite families discovered that the French families had left the country . . . taking with them their little Alaouite servant whom they had bought for ten years, and for whom they had paid a lot of money.

Parents have spent years searching for their stolen children. One such case came to light in April, 1951, when Mrs. Mariam Ahmad Bakuchi reported to the British Agency in Sharjah, on the Persian Gulf, that two years previously her 14-year-old daughter had been kidnapped from Lubai. After a long and fruitless search the mother found that the girl had been sent to Saudi Arabia by way of Buraimi, a traditional route. The Ruler of Dubai gave her a personal letter addressed to King Saud but an official in Riyadh to whom she presented this letter tore it up, unread. Ejected from the building, the woman went on pilgrimage to Mecca and discovered that her daughter was living as a slave in the home of Abdur Rehman bin Rawaf. She pleaded with him to release her daughter but was told she would be flogged if she made any more trouble. She importuned various Saudi authorities but nobody would listen to her complaint, and poverty forced her to return home. As far as is known, she never did succeed in freeing her daughter.

Buraimi Oasis in 1955 was a neutral zone, administered under an agreement between the British and Saudi governments. At the time it was well known in Arabia that Buraimi was the staging point for a brisk traffic in slaves heading for Saudi, a fact brought to the notice of the Anti-Slavery Society by an officer of the Trucial Scouts, an Arab desert military force led by British officers.[5]

Under the Buraimi Agreement each side was allowed three aircraft flights a month to supply the small army contingents; these planes were forbidden to carry civilian passengers and could be used for no purpose other than military supply. But the Trucial Scouts officer noticed that when the Saudi aircraft was about to leave, usually at dusk, trucks loaded with people arrived in a rush and the people would be hurried aboard the plane, which took off at once. A Saudi official told the Englishman that these were Buraimi residents going to visit relations. But investigation showed that the passengers were slaves who had arrived by truck from Dubai and were then flown to Saudi Arabia. It seemed probable that the British Political Agency was aware of the traffic.

The aircraft were piloted by Americans, and the British officer asked one of them if he knew what was going on. The American, who was paid a large salary, had been told that his job was to fly the plane and not to ask questions and this, he said, he was doing. Each plane carried thirty to forty slaves on a flight; over a year this meant up to 2,000 slaves. The use of Buraimi as an air slavery boarding point ended when the two-nation army contingents were removed, but while it lasted the profits were great for all concerned.

In 1955 a specific case of a Mecca pilgrim selling a servant into slavery in Saudi Arabia became world news. A Tuareg of the French Sudan (Mali), a chief named Mohammed Ali ag Attaher, told his servant, whom he had taken to the holy cities, that he must work for the Governor of Jedda to earn money for his fare home. The servant, Awd el Joud, aged 16, agreed to this, but then found that he was receiving no wages and had in fact been bought by the son of the Governor of Jedda. At great risk he escaped and later, in Mali, he

[5]*Anti-Slavery Reporter*, June, 1960.

told his story to a white priest, Father David Traore. He spoke of the slave markets in Saudi Arabia, saying that they were in all the big towns, with sales about 5 p.m. daily.

An even more disturbing report came from the French Ambassador to Saudi Arabia. It was sent as a dispatch to the Minister of Foreign Affairs, Paris. In July, 1956, Pastor Emmanual La Gravieré, Councillor of the Assembly of the French Union, made its contents public in an address at the annual meeting of the Anti-Slavery Society, London, which published the ambassador's report.

He disclosed the presence of slaves in Saudi Arabia and the trade in Negroes "carried off from their native land by means of many tricks" to be sold among the rich people of Mecca, Riyadh and Jedda. Merchants living in Jedda or Mecca sent Saudi Arabians of Senegalese origin as emissaries to recruit people from the villages of the Sudan, the High-Volta or of the Niger, notably around Timbuktu. "They pose as Moslem missionaries entrusted with the delicate mission of guiding their compatriots to the Holy Places of Islam to make the pilgrimage and to be instructed in the Koran in Arabic," the ambassador wrote. "Moslem natives fall into this trap. Men, women, and children are then transported to the shores of the Red Sea at Port Sudan or Suakin. Having crossed the Red Sea in chartered dhows the Negroes disembark at Lith [a little port 200 kilometres south of Jedda.] They are then declared to be illegal immigrants and are loaded into lorries and taken to Jedda where they are imprisoned."

The following day a Saudi Arabian merchant arrived and collected the Negroes from the police. The sale took place at once and the slaves then vanished into the houses of their masters, which, the ambassador stated, "they would never leave as free men."

He reported that the price varied according to sex and age. A girl under fifteen years was sold at £200 – £400; a man under 40 for £150, an old woman £40.

"On condition that they accept their lot, renounce all idea of freedom, and submit body and soul to the desires of their masters, they are assured of a material existence superior to that which they could have got in their village in Africa. The men can rise to posts of trust, such as steward, chauffeur, bodyguard. The women who become mothers are treated in practice as wives. . . . The local demand continues to be strong. Slaves constitute an important element in the social organisation; the pride of the Arab hinders him from performing a number of tasks considered as servile and degrading. So, with the connivance of the Saudi Arabian authorities the ancient trade in black-ivory is perpetuated in our time in spite of the international conventions. . . . The paradox reaches its climax following a recent speech of the Saudi Arabian delegate to the U.N. on the question of Tunisia [then under French rule]. A nation which tolerates on its soil the sale of human beings — French natives under the circumstances — whose religious sentiments have been exploited without scruple, seem far from well placed to attack France in the name of the rights of man."

La Gravieré, himself an investigator on slavery in Saudi Arabia, met a high-ranking French civil servant responsible for seeing that Africans from the French West African colonies — those who had made voluntary pilgrimages to Saudi Arabia — got safely onto ships for the return journey to Dakar. He was approached by an African, Aval Yattara, who said that he had been invited by a Mohammed Ali al Attaher to go with other Africans from French Sudan on a pilgrimage to the Islamic holy places. When he arrived at Jedda, after a long and complicated trip, he was "placed" in the palace of a Saudi Prince, Emir Abdallah, while waiting to continue to Mecca. He was lodged and fed and in return he had to work hard. Yattara thought all this was normal until the day when he was taken to the market and sold. He escaped and sought refuge at the French Embassy, where he showed papers proving his story, and gave the names of four other people sold at the same time. He demanded his repatriation, but the ambassador decided that it was impossible to place him on the official list of those to be repatriated. He feared reprisals from the Saudi Government, for the owner of this slave was none other than the Saudi Arabian Minister of Interior. However, Yattara was promised that if he managed to get secretly onto the ship for Dakar the necessary papers would be arranged for him before departure. At the last minute the man took fright and did not embark, and the French official told La Gravieré that from information received it seemed that had he tried to do so, he would have been beaten by the Saudi police, who had been notified of his action.

"Saudi Arabia seems to be the most guilty as far as 'classical' slavery is concerned," wrote *The Economist* on August 4, 1956. "Detailed information given to the United Nations shows that the Africans sold in Mecca originally made the voyage under the impression that they were undertaking a pilgrimage. Young girls were generally stolen from villages in agreement with the heads of the villages. No convincing denial to this dreadful accusation has been given by the Saudi Arabian Government."

La Gravieré's information, widely publicized in France in the late 1950s, brought strong condemnation of the slave trade from African Moslems. The Head Iman of the Sudan said:

". . . . We intend to make our beliefs respected and not to allow them to be exploited. . . . We completely disapprove of slavery, even more so since the ultimate gesture of our Prophet was to free all his slaves just before his death, and to inspire all Moslems to do the same. . . . Listening to our conscience, and imitating our Prophet, we condemn and denounce all those who follow the dishonest route of a shameful and criminal trade."

But by the 1960s slavery in Arabia was flourishing as never before. Much of the Arabian peninsula was growing wealthy from oil money and slaves were considered not only a good investment but a socially desirable commodity. James Morris, a correspondent for the London *Times,* had recognized this in 1956. "As an industry and social institution, slavery is still important to the Saudis, unlikely though it may sometimes seem amidst the hygiene of the oil towns or the grand office blocks of Jedda. Among rich men a young girl slave is an acceptable gift. Among merchants, a stout negro is a useful piece of equipment."[6]

As a medical officer, Herbert Pritzke spent nearly a decade in Saudi Arabia, and lived for a time with a tribe whose Emir was required to supply seventy slaves every year to the king. The doctors of the Health Office, which employed Pritzke, had to report on the health of the slave convoys which came through on the way to the capital. On the birthday of the prophet Mohammad the Emir, as a special favor, allowed Dr. Pritzke to buy a white girl from a merchant. He put her on a plane out of the country.[7]

Pritzke showed some enterprise in getting the girl out of Arabia but dhow captains were showing, as always, even more shrewdness in getting slaves into Arabia. A favorite ploy was to enlist Africans as members of the ship's crew, promising them a well-paid, well-fed life at sea — only to deliver them into the hands of a slave dealer at one of Arabia's ports. Sometimes an Arab traveler would hire an African servant and pay him a wage; but the moment they arrived in Arabia he, too, was off to the slave market. Both these practices were believed to be prevalent in 1975.

In the House of Lords on July 14, 1960, Lord Maugham, who had disclosed so much about Tuareg slavery, reported the changing conditions in Saudi Arabia under the impetus of new wealth. "Vice is unrestrained and the means to gratify unusual lusts can easily be procured by money. There are sheikhs who can only achieve sexual satisfaction with young children. Slaves are often horribly abused for pleasure or mutilated as a punishment and the castration of young boys is practised."

One of the most disturbing stories of slavery was told in 1957 by Dr. Claudia Fayein, briefly referred to in Chapter I. Mother of several children, Dr. Fayein qualified as a doctor in 1940 and undertook a medical mission to the Yemen in 1951. A high-ranking diplomat from Saudi Arabia wished to buy a slave girl from a Yemeni prince as a gift for his own prince and his direct government superior, with whom he was traveling in Yemen. This prince was a son of King Ibn Saud. The price had been agreed upon (£700), but before the deal could go through the girl had to be medically examined, and Dr. Fayein was the only doctor available. She had already spent a year in

---

[6]James Morris, *The Market of Seleukia.* (London: Faber & Faber, 1957).
[7]Herbert Pritzke, *Bedouin Doctor.* (London: Weidenfeld & Nicholson, 1957).

the Yemen and knew that for a girl to be worth so much money she had to be white. Dr. Fayein was collected by one of the prince's aides, who took her to the palace and sent for the slave girl. The doctor, assessing the girl's age as fifteen, considered that she had a pretty enough body but her face was "scowling, hard and common." At first the girl was merely puzzled and apprehensive but the Prince's presence seemed to reassure her.

She let herself be examined but then apparently understood the purpose of the inspection and protested. When the prince tried to calm her and persuade her, she became violent and the prince held her down by force. He wanted to know if the girl was free of venereal disease. Scared and shamed, the girl kept on struggling against the prince's hold and Dr. Fayein was as outraged as the girl. She said, when disclosing the episode years later, that it was the slave girl's wounded expression which made her break her Hippocratic oath.

The girl was, in fact, quite healthy, but Dr. Fayein was able to say with perfect honesty that the skin of her arms and legs was slightly grainy as the result of poor vitamin balance in her diet. She wrote this on the certificate. Soon after she returned home the Yemeni prince arrived, bringing with him the Saudi Prince and the diplomat who wanted to buy the girl as a present for him. All deeply disturbed, they fired questions at Dr. Fayein. Was the girl's condition syphilitic? Was it contagious? Could it be cured? If so, how long would this take and would the trouble recur? Dr. Fayein gave them a description of all the symptoms, some of them horrible, of pellagra, the vitamin deficiency disease from which the girl suffered. The deception worked; the girl was not sold and the Yemeni prince renewed his attachment to her; this, Dr. Fayein thought, was at least preferable to the trauma of being sold and still further exploited.

It was never clear where the Yemeni prince's concubine had come from, but there is no secret about the origin of other slaves.

An editorial writer in the *West African Pilot* of October 31, 1961, protested about the Nigerians held in Saudi Arabia and the Sudan and forced to work as slaves. "The Nigerian Government acted well in repatriating dozens of pilgrims without support, knowing the fate which hundreds of compatriots bought by rich Arabs had suffered, and now they are lost forever in the Arabian deserts. The Government should do all it can to find these men and to save them. Slavery is tolerated in Saudi Arabia and we know that a good number of Nigerians who left during the last ten years for Mecca have never come back. It is easy to guess what happened to them. The Nigerian Government must be certain that no pilgrim leaves the country without having the means to cover his expenses. Most of the pilgrims going to Mecca are so carried away by enthusiasm, that they do not think of anything other than the means to go there. Unfortunately Allah does not give them a magic carpet to bring them home again and they soon find themselves in the slave market of Mecca. . . ."

The principal slave market in Mecca — the Suk el Abd — is a narrow street; the tall houses on either side allow little daylight to reach the roadway. Against the houses are stone benches — really display counters — on which until recently the slaves were displayed for sale. The crowd moved slowly past, scanning the slaves and discussing them with the dealers. Mecca in its heyday as a slave market also had street auctioneers — the *dallal* — who specialized in the sale of slave girls. Always in touch with potential buyers and sellers, they were the middlemen who arranged sales and guided the prospective buyer to the secret doors which hid the slave girls from the common eye.

The white Circassian slaves, male and female, coming from Constantinople, were very expensive and also were never sold in an open market in Mecca. Sound, secure references were needed to gain access to a display of *these* slaves.

The Lagos *Morning Post,* taking up the story of Nigerians being sold in Saudi Arabia, quoted a report by the Anti-Slavery Society, which had revealed "A continual traffic of slave children taken from Nigeria to Arabia" and a Saudi Arabian denial of the report. The *Morning Post* saw the denial as an attempt to hide the truth.

> Arabia, unlike Nigeria, is not completely part of the civilised world, and because of this Saudi Arabia, the Yemen, the Sultanates of Oman and Aden, in fact most of Arabia, still recognise the legal status of slavery. . . . All requests for information sent by the United Nations to Saudi Arabia concerning slavery in its territory have been greeted with oriental indifference, and totally ignored. Apart from this confirmatory silence on the part of Saudi Arabia, there is official proof within the country that slavery and the slave trade are flourishing there. The traffic of African children was confirmed by an investigation concerning the French-speaking African countries. How can one not believe that the young Nigerian "workers" there are not in fact slaves? For example, it was noted that the method used in these cases was to send Mohammadan Africans to Africa in order to recruit these children to line the pockets of the merchants of Jedda and Mecca. . . . Is it not logical to conclude that if these young Africans from all corners of Western Africa were sold there, that our own young "workers" in Arabia have met the same fate?

There had already been Arab corroboration of the slavers' trick of escorting "pilgrims" to Mecca and turning them into slaves from no less a figure than Mohammad Heikal, one of President Nasser's most trusted counselors and editor of the Cairo daily *Al Ahram*. Haikal reported an incident which had profoundly disturbed him.[8]

---

[8]*Al Ahram,* January 27, 1961.

If I had not personally heard the discussion between Abdul Kader al Alam, Minister for Foreign Affairs of Libya and Sheikh Mohammed Mehdi, a member of the official delegation of Mali to the Casablanca Conference, I would have thought that this story was pure invention. The discussion in question concerned a Mali citizen living now in exile in Libya. . . . The conversation aroused the interest of all those who were there. Sheikh Mehdi declared, "The man in question is wanted by my country. He was the chief of a Mali tribe. A little before my country's independence, he called upon the members of his tribe to undertake the pilgrimage to Mecca. Many listened to him. Among them were men and a large number of women accompanied by their children. After much excitement they arrived at Mecca, and there they were sold to many slave traders. After having gained money by selling his own people this man left Mecca, and instead of returning to Mali, he went to Libya where he opened a business. An exchange of letters took place between the Ministry of Foreign Affairs of Libya and the same in Mali [to have him extradited] without any result until now."

The following year other Egyptian newspapers were protesting about slavery in Saudi Arabia, and on March 2, 1962, *Al Goumhouriya* published the text of a telegram sent by a Saudi trade-union leader, Nasires Said, to King Ibn Saud. It concerned the case of a workman, Marzouk, a former slave freed by his master, Mohammad Bin Ahmad al Dansawi. This merchant was asking 50,000 ryals for Marzouk's wife and children, and Marzouk had publicly asked the workmen of Jedda to collect the sum necessary to redeem them. Said's telegram to the King said: "The slave merchants claim that the slave-trade is permitted by Islam, but Islam and every other divine religion rejects this. We ask that the farce of one human being selling another should cease, because it is a disgrace which ridicules Saudi Arabia before other nations." Trade unions have no status in Saudi Arabia and Nasires Said had to flee the country to escape the anger of the Saudi authorities, but he published, in Cairo, a little book on the conditions of slave workers in Arabia. It is believed that Marzouk's wife and children were sold to a man from Riyadh.

At this time some Saudi princes — about twenty from among the 5,000 in Saudi Arabia — attempted a pro-Nasser coup in their own country but it was abortive and they had to escape hurriedly to Egypt. On February 27, 1962, over Cairo radio they made an appeal in the name of the Liberal Front for Reform in Saudi Arabia:

We consider it our sacred duty to make the international public aware of the question of negro and white slavery in Saudi Arabia. . . . All humanitarian organizations must intensify their campaigns and their protests to denounce and put an end to the evil of negro and white slave traffic. Agents go as far afield as Africa, Iraq and Iran to find their human merchandise, which they bring back to Saudi Arabia. The slave is often put to work for oil companies and his wages paid to his master. . . .

Slaves were not only imported from Iraq but from Qatar, from Ethiopia and Somalia, from Iran, Africa and Asia, and often even from Europe. These European girls were first of all employed to work in the night clubs in Beirut and Damascus, where they were chosen, without their knowledge, by the more important slave traders. From here they went the way of harems, brothels and other markets in Arabia. The richest merchants and tribes in the traffic included the el Dowasir tribe, operating in the northern part of the desert and the region of Qatar; the al Mourra tribe operating around the Buraimi Oasis; the al Manasir tribe operating mainly in the region of Buraimi; as well as the al Dohm, al Nabit and al Habbar tribes. The best known route was from Doubai, Muscat, Buraimi, Al Has, Riyadh. The main slave traders following this route were Ibn Gruraib, Al Mirri, Jabou Ibn Hadfa and Ibn Ard Rabbo. These merchants made seasonal trips to Dubai and Muscat and bought back slaves in groups of fifty or sixty at a time. One of these merchants told how people were taken from villages scheduled for a raid. The slavers would arrange a kind of fair a little way out of the village, and musicians, jugglers and dancers would be on hand to entertain the villagers. Unknown to them the slavers had struck a deal with a neighboring tribe to raid their "enemies" during the show. The captives would be handed over to the dealer and the sheikh of the raiding tribe would be paid for his work. The dealer then sold his slaves either privately, if he had standing orders, or openly in the markets, such as that at Meecca, and called Dakkar al Abd — the "slave stage" — on which slaves were presented by their seller, attached six or seven together.

A group of young girls was taken from the region of Qatar[9] and among them was the niece of a well-known merchant, Ibn Maktoum. She was sold twice at Al Hassa and later transferred to Riyadh, where she was sold to the royal family. During this time her family was making inquiries in the desert. Finding out what had happened, the family sent a group of 120 armed men to Al Hassa to demand her release by the Saudi authorities. A telegram was sent to Riyadh, and the young girl was finally returned to her family.

Occasionally, slavers have been punished. Mohammad Hussein, a trader who provided King Saud with young male and female slaves whom he brought from Iraq and Iran, was caught by the Iraqi police, tried and sentenced to ten years in prison. At the moment of his arrest he had fifty young girls he was taking to sell in Riyadh.

---

[9]The Sheikhs of Qatar brought slaves in their retinue on visits to Britain for the Coronation of Queen Elizabeth in 1953 and also on their visit in 1958 (*Anti-Slavery Reporter*, March, 1962).

In 1962 a Saudi Arabian reported to the Anti-Slavery Society the existence in Jedda of a place known in Arabic as El-Rabatt, roughly equivalent to "Alms Houses." In fact, El-Rabatt is a place for sending slaves no longer useful to their masters. Visiting this building to leave some money for the slaves' benefit, the Saudi met a woman whom he had known well several years before. A white slave, she had been bought by one of Jedda's richest men as a gift for his young son, whose children she bore. The couple had six children, and occasionally the woman visited Cairo where her children were sent for their education. Her husband accused her of running away in Cairo with another man, an unjust charge, according to the Saudi. The result was that she was escorted to Jedda and "imprisoned" in El-Rabatt. "The last time I saw this woman she was still living there, not allowed to see any of her children for the rest of her life," the Saudi told the Society. Outspoken, even if anonymously, he said that King Ibn Saud had 3,000 slaves of his own, and urged democratic governments to force an end to slavery.[10]

On November 6, 1962, four days after his appointment as Prime Minister of Saudi Arabia, Prince Faisal issued a "Ten-Point Programme" of slave reforms. The tenth is:

> The attitude of the Shari'a towards slavery and its keen interest in liberating slaves is well known. It is also known that any slavery existing at the present time fails to fulfill many of the Shari'a's conditions laid down by Islam for slavery. Ever since Saudi Arabia's foundation [in 1922] it has been faced with this problem of slaves and slavery and has striven by all gradual means to abolish slavery, first by prohibiting the importation of slaves and imposing penalties . . . and later by prohibiting the sale or purchase of slaves. The Government now finds a favourable opportunity to announce the absolute abolition of slavery. . . . "

But this decree did not, in fact, end slavery and "slave identity cards" were still issued in 1963. Reluctance to end slavery was understandable enough in psychological terms. It was difficult for men who had used the services of slaves for years to surrender them; the attitudes of centuries could not be changed overnight. Three years after the Saudi Arabian edict the United Nations published — in the Economic and Social Council document on slavery of July 16, 1965 — an extract of a communication from the Anti-Slavery Society which charged that King Saud himself still had slaves.

> Saudi Arabia was the last country in Arabia to decree the abolition of slavery . . . . Saudi Arabia has never published a census of its population, even

---

[10]*Anti-Slavery Reporter*, March, 1962.

less of its slaves, and their respective numbers can only be evaluatee approximately. The total population is estimated to be 8 million, and an important Saudi Arabian revealed to a European traveller that the slave population was about 250,000 . . . [although] in 1963 the Saudi Arabia Government paid £1,785,000 compensation for 1,682 freed slaves . . . following the Royal Decree of November 1962. It is known that Prince Faisal, the real leader of Saudi Arabia, does not own any slaves and that he had freed those whom he had before promulgation of the Decree of 1962. It is also known that King Saud owns many hundreds of slaves as do many others of high rank.

The bulletin of the Anti-Slavery Society told the story of twelve Baluchee slaves owned personally by King Saud. They conspired to escape, and collected enough money to buy two camels and food to cross the desert. Upon their escape their overseer immediately sent guards in chase. Nine runaways were decapitated in the desert where they were captured, and three were taken for decapitation in the public square in Riyadh as an example to others.

The following year, 1966, Sir Douglas Glover, President of the Anti-Slavery Society, attempted in his annual report to find in history the reasons for the continuation of slavery in the period 1945 to 1966. He believed that this period resembled that of 1834 to 1890 [that is, before the date of the Brussels Convention and the establishment of the International Bureau for Slavery] in that they were both periods during which slavery was condemned, without any effective measures for its abolition being put into practice. If slavery had developed after the First World War, it was because the new convention of 1926, replacing that of Brussels in 1890, did not provide methods for repressing the trade. In this sense, the progress achieved by the Committee of Experts of the League of Nations between 1933 and 1939 was swept away by the upheavals of the Second World War and by the change of administration in many countries, mainly Africa. In addition, the unanimous resolution by the United Nations in 1956 to outlaw slavery had resulted in a Convention on Slavery which only 62 of the 115 member countries of the U.N. signed in 1965. [Saudi Arabia did not sign.]

The last twenty years had been "a sorry story," Sir Douglas said. "There is no doubt that as a result of the growing richness of the Arab Peninsula, owing to the discovery of petrol in regions where slavery is an accepted practice, and hwzteeen fr thousands of years — and yes, it must be admitted, the slave was usually well treated — slaves have become a status symbol and their price has gone up drastically. . . . Consequently, there is an ever-increasing fleet from Nigeria, Mauritania, Mali and other parts of the world to the Arab Peninsula, because people are willing to pay a much higher price than before."

From where does this need come, particularly in Arabs, to possess slaves?

Saudi Arabia: Slavery As Part of a Lifestyle

The French journalist Eric Rouleau, investigating slavery in Saudi Arabia in 1966, interviewed one of the nation's mos important businessmen, Ali Jugali. The Saudi told Rouleau that for practical reasons he was opposed to Koranic interpretations which allow abuses — such as the institution of the harem — of the Holy Book. "What a waste of human force," he said, "to relegate to the harem many hundreds of thousands of women and thus keep them in a state of slavery — all this eliminates a good part of the potential labour force which the country needs."[11]

Rouleau analyzed the "key problem" of Saudi Arabia as "the lack of a labour force without which all the oil in the world cannot create the basis of a modern economy." Rouleau believed that slaves were an integral part of Saudi Arabia's society, more integral perhaps than the power of religion, which he considered relaxing. He saw a dissolution of morals; as evidence of this he pointed out that "of all countries in the world, the Wahabite Kingdom is the greatest importer of pornographic films."

It is likely that, fifteen years after Rouleau's observations, Saudi Arabia is still the principal importer of slaves. Officially, slavery does not exist; indeed, it is outlawed. But the black market thrives, and since the tremendous increase in oil wealth in 1974 — when prices were more than quadrupled — more money has been available for slaves. It must be stated that in some cases these slaves are not slaves within the meaning of United Nations legislation. European women procured for immoral purposes, consenting and highly paid, and allowed to leave at the end of a contract, are hardly the same as those black women lured to the Arabian sub-continent by promises of easy money, and then prevented by one means or another from returning home. But Africans are still tricked into making the pilgrimage to Mecca and then sold into slavery; Moslem boys from the Indian sub-continent are still stolen, to disappear into Arabia; European girls vanish — Geneva is a good hunting ground. The dhow slavers have virtually disappeared — to be replaced by modern ships and, more frequently, airplanes. The long-distance plane is the slaver's dream — from source to market in one hop.

Any man able to afford to buy slaves could now equally well afford to pay normal employees; that is, he could openly advertise for servants or staff, pay them a wage and accommodate them, and after some contractual term return them to their own land. Some Saudi Arabians and other Arabs of the sub-continent do this. But this approach has no real attraction; it is neither as exciting nor as satisfying as buying the human commodity. Habits die hard, and these habits are thousands of years old.

One of these habits, sexual activity, is fundamental, and its relation to slavery is well expressed by yet another desert traveler, Wendell Phillips.

---

[11] *Le Monde*, June 23, 1966.

"The survival of slavery and existence of concubinage in parts of the Arabian peninsula is to a large extent due to the specific need to co-habit with non-circumcised, sexually keen women, who echo the man's desire and derive pleasure from love-making."[12]

Bertram Thomas, for many years advisor to the Sultan of Oman, could explain from experience why the Arabs were reluctant to relinquish slave trading. "Within Arabia slavery flourishes with the full support of public opinion and any extraneous authority interfering becomes odious. . . . It is a vested interest of immemorial respectability. . . . Slavery is a traditional part of the social structure. It is congenial. The peninsular Arabs are far too proud to work as servants . . . so that the well-to-do have either to do the work themselves or work as slaves. That is why, among a poor people, having little more than a subsistence agriculture, all attempts at suppression have failed."[13]

Thomas does not explain how the poor people could afford big money for slaves. He was writing before oil wealth, but after its discovery he would have been forced to note that suppression of slavery was still extremely difficult. "In the unabatement of slavery," he wrote, "Arabia has been false to her prophet."

A recent student of slavery, Jonathan Derrick, considers that in view of the experience of other countries ". . . it would be fantastic; if all traces of Saudi Arabia's widespread slavery had vanished . . . and all danger of clandestine slave-trading removed; and the problem of 'white slavery' very probably remains serious."[14]

At this point it is well worth going back more than 150 years to the travels of Jean Louis Burckhardt, one of the very few Europeans to see slavery and its effects in both Africa, the source, and in Arabia, the market. This remarkably courageous Swiss explorer possessed not only acute perception and observation but vision as well. Living and traveling in the slave hunting grounds of Africa and in many parts of Arabia throughout the years 1809 to 1817, Burckhardt produced seven massive volumes of his experiences for the African Society of London, which had helped to finance his journeys.[15]

His comments on the slave trade are particularly valuable because of his unique opportunities to observe it. In preparation for his great journeys, he spent two and a half years in Syria learning to be an Arab. He spoke Arabic as if it were his native tongue, dressed as an Arab or Turk — the region was part

---

[12] *Unknown Oman*, London, 1960.
[13] *The Arabs*, London, 1938.
[14] Jonathan Derrick, *Africa's Slaves Today*, London, 1975.
[15] He died of dysentery in Cairo in 1817, at the age of 32. Despite his short life, his accomplishments were prodigious. He was, for instance, the first European to enter Petra, and he was the discoverer of the colossal figures at Abu Simbel. His books, all published posthumously, deserve to be better known.

of the Ottoman Empire — and posed as a poor Syrian sheikh with powerful friends. No Arab ever penetrated his life-saving disguise.

From the beginning of his travels in Egypt and the Sudan, Burckhardt recognized the African-Arabian trade as being a much more serious problem than the Atlantic trade. It was bigger, more brutal and, unlike African slavery in the Americas, it was partly a religious perversion.

When the Arab slavers were under the observation of Europeans, such as Burton and Livingstone, they were often more circumspect than usual, but they showed no inhibitions in front of Sheikh Ibrahim-Burckhardt. In Cairo, Burckhardt had heard slave traders claim that the chastity of the most beautiful girls was always respected. He found out that this was so only in public places; in the desert or bush the traders became diabolically lustful. During a journey from the Sudan interior to the port of Suakin, the caravan usually camped in one large circle as protection against attack from bandits; within this arena Burckhardt watched "scenes of the most shameless indecency." He decided that few girl slaves older than ten reached their destination as virgins. Throughout the night and these licentious orgies the adult male Negroes lay powerless, shackled in irons.

Burckhardt saw many a slaver sell the "use" of his female slaves to fellow dealers or to other merchants traveling with the caravan.

In the deserts the caravans stopped for a drink of water about nine in the morning and twice during the afternoon, around four and six. A slaver with many captives would fill the large wooden food bowl with water and the slaves were made to kneel down and drink from it like cattle. This practice prevented the wastage which might occur by pouring individual allowances. Burckhardt often likens the life of slaves to that of animals. This was especially so in Cairo, a sink of iniquity to the Swiss. The thriving slave market sickened him. He often saw gangs of slaves driven through the city to the market, where they lived in fetid filth and abject misery, crowded together "as if in sheep-pens." He was particularly sorry for the girls and young women herded through the streets. Wearing nothing but a piece of tattered cloth around their waists they could only endure the torments of the street boys who poked them or pulled at them, all the time shouting obscenely.

Burckhardt wrote a long and vivid description of the great Arab general merchandise market at Shendi in Nubia, where slaves were the most expensive and desirable items. He estimated that the Shendi dealers sold about 5,000 slaves annually: half going to Suakin on the Red Sea coast, 1,500 to Egypt and the rest to parts of the Sudan or to the Bedouin tribes east of Shendi. He saw many children of four and five forcibly separated from their parents and among the slave girls he found many *mukhaeyt* — girls whose vagina had been sewn up by the Arab slavers or market merchants. This operation may have taken place years before their sale so that the flesh had "agonisingly joined up" as Burckhardt put it. The girls were left with a small orifice for urinating; their menstrual distress can be imagined. "Girls in this state," Burckhardt wrote, "are worth more than others; they are usually given to the favourite mistress of the purchaser and are often suffered to remain in this state during the whole of their life." But a good many others remained stitched only until after sale. With their virginity so well established they brought a high price from the Arab buyer who would have his new possession opened up to the extent he found most satisfying and then proceed to deflower her.

Safe in his guise as a Moslem, Burckhardt achieved a feat which few Christian travelers before or since have been able to emulate — he entered the Islamic holy city of Mecca. He was shocked by the number of pilgrims who died from exhaustion, starvation or illness incurred during their pilgrimage. Equally he was horrified by "the grossest depravity . . . indecencies and criminal acts" and by the presence of thousands of prostitutes, including slave girls forced into harlotry by their masters and many high-class prostitutes who had come from Egypt for the rich pickings available during the pilgrimage. He was perturbed, too, to find that despite all the laws of Islam against alcohol certain shops in Mecca did a brisk trade in strong drink. That this could happen in Mecca seemed hypocritical to Burckhardt. Other pilgrims and the Meccan people themselves broke holy law by gambling, and they indulged in sexual perversions. They would say to Burckhardt, "God has made the Arabs great sinners but he has bestowed upon us also the virtue of easy repentance."

In Mecca, Medina and Jedda Burckhardt saw the worst of horrors — the thousands of helpless, hopeless slaves in the market places. In Mecca many of the Abyssinian slaves were bought by Turkish Moslems who had come to Mecca on pilgrimage. The Swiss records that many pilgrims pretended to bargain with slave dealers so that they would have an excuse to view the slave girls naked and in private.

Many of the slave men and boys had been turned into Moslems, nominally at least, by circumcision, but they received no instruction in religion and knew nothing of the Koran. Still, the "making" of a pagan into a Moslem was considered laudable, and circumcision technically completed the conversion.

Among the many slavers Burckhardt knew personally was one of the most evil and rapacious in slaving history, Haj Ali Bornaway, whose three pilgrimages to Mecca had won him great renown. This voluptuary, who read the Koran while he rested during the hottest part of the day, lived only for vice. It was well known that he had sold his own cousin in the slave market of Medina. This woman, having gone on pilgrimage from Bornu to Mecca, happened to meet Ali in the holy city. Short of concubines, he married her — it is permissible for a man to marry his cousin in Moslem countries. In

Medina, Bornaway ran out of money; so he sold his cousin-wife to some Egyptians, and she, unable to prove that she was a free woman, was forced to submit.

With his deep knowledge of the Arabs and the Africans, Burckhardt pondered for a long time on the slave problem and wrote that the ultimate solution was the education of Africans in their own country and by their own countrymen, rather than as formerly — by Europeans. Only then would Negroes be able to resist and repel the Moslem traders.

Probably he would not be surprised to know that 150 years after he made this observation Negroes were still not wholly able to "resist and repel." The master-slave relationship dies hard.

VII
The "Official" Attitude

Islam's attitude to slavery is ambiguous and ambivalent and can hardly be anything else. The Koran forbids slavery and introduced the new idea that it is highly meritorious to set slaves free This is straightforward enough. But, says the Moslem, you cannot set slaves free unless you first own slaves — therefore slavery is sanctioned by God and almost certainly directly commanded by Him.

If this appears to oversimplify the issue then it is the way that scholars, theologians as well as slave owners and most ordinary Moslems interpret the Koran.

A remarkable paradox arises, as the Imam of the Sha Jehan Mosque, London, implied in a sermon in June, 1962. "Islam is the only true religion to have made the emancipation of slaves a matter of great virtue, thus laying down the basis for the abolition of slavery. But, very strangely, it is the only religion accused of perpetuating this institution. . . ."

The Imam was not conceding that this accusation had some truth; he was being entirely defensive, alleging that the world at large was "unfair" to Islam. Even more defensively, some Moslem scholars endeavor to prove that Islam has never admitted to slavery. Their argument runs along these lines: Islam, of all religions, is the one which raises the human being to the highest possible position. God, in the Koran, honors man and considers him his own viceroy on earth, just as He asserts that He has created everything in the universe for man's service, including the sun, the stars and all creation. This bounty is not limited to those who believe in Islam but to the whole human race, since it derives from the same source. This means that the spirit of Islam forbids slavery; if it did not, then man is no better than a chattel or animal without any respect or honor, and this would be a contradiction within Islam itself, an unacceptable state of affairs, since Islam is claimed to be the only logical religion. Therefore, it can be said that slavery is forbidden in Islam and, being forbidden, has not taken place.

But Islam *did* condone slavery, and the Koran itself contains many verses in which are given the conditions of slaves and the recommended relationship between them and their masters. A former Imam of the Islamic Cultural Centre in Britain, Mr. H. Ghoraba, says it is undeniable that although the prophet Mohammad and most of his close associates had freed their slaves, some of them had slaves until death.[1] "We cannot claim that those Companions had not understood the spirit of Islam or that they understood it but neglected to act in accordance because of their passion or pride in the possession of slaves. Therefore, we have to say that Islam admitted slavery in certain cases, but this admission does not imply that Islam is reactionary or contradictory."

A great number of Moslem thinkers have defended Islam on other lines. They have agreed that Islam does permit slavery, although it does not establish it or consider it as a part of its teaching, and they have endeavored to redeem this admission by showing the kindness advocated by Islam in the treatment of slaves. They have drawn the attention of mankind to the verses of the Koran and the traditions which define and state the rights of those slaves, denied or neglected by their masters before Islam. They say that slaves in those times had no rights as human beings but were treated like animals and perhaps even worse.

Mr. Ghoraba says that humanity ought to complain not of the Prophet but rather of the Arab masters and of the Roman masters who used to drive their slaves into planned battles so that they might amuse themselves with the scene of slaves killing each other. "In this they arouse our profound scorn for this community [Rome] which was considered the most advanced society of its period, while contrasting it with the humanity of the laws of Islam."

Mr. Ghoraba and others say that the teaching of kindliness towards slaves is asserted in many traditions emanating from the Koran and hadiths. For instance, the Prophet asked the master not to hurt the feelings of his slaves; he could not say "My male slave" or "My female slave" but "My man" and "My girl."

Similarly, the Prophet said, "Your slaves are your brothers," and commanded the master, because of this, to feed and clothe his slave with the same kind of food and clothing as his own and not to ask the slave to do anything that was beyond his ability, "but if you do, you must help him."

Islam states, too, that the master has no right to punish or inflict pain on his slave, except to deal with him in the way he would treat his own sons. Even

---

[1] In a sermon at the Cultural Centre, April 8, 1955.

to make the slave act in "a good way" the master could not inflict punishment. Forsaking or neglecting his slave and thus causing his death was blameworthy; if the master murdered his slave his life was to be taken also.

The Prophet married his cousin Zainab to his former slave Zaid, to prove that the slave has the same honor as the noblest free person. In addition, he chose the son of Zaid to lead his army, which included the first two among his Companions, infinitely superior in other ways to the army commander. Again, the Prophet told Moslems to obey and help the ruler, even if he was a slave, as long as the ruler obeyed God.

All these injunctions and acts are necessarily founded on the existence of slaves in Moslem society, so again there is the assumption that slavery existed as of right.

At this point the apologists for Islam's attitude to slavery generally go on the attack with invidious comparisons. Mr. Ghoraba's sermon might well be quoted:

> Why is Islam criticised because of its admission of slavery when it was admitted by nearly all societies throughout the world at that time. It was admitted not by the secular laws only as it was in Egypt and Persia, but also by the two great religions of that time, Judaism and Christianity. The Bible had permitted the lender to take the borrower as slave if the latter failed to refund his debt. And it is admitted in the Bible too that the father may sell his daughter and may even sell himself. These are things about which Christianity had kept silent but which were forbidden by Islam later. Admittedly Christianity had told its followers to treat all creatures kindly, but about slavery and the rights of a slave to establish his right to freedom, no word has been said. It is admitted by many Christians that their religion did not discuss the problem in a positive way. If so, why did Christian people attack Islam on this issue? Islam tried to reform a condition which was inherited from the old days, and for this humanity should praise Islam rather than attack it. Meditation upon the policy of Islam would prove that Islam came to abolish slavery in spite of its admission. Slavery before Islam was like a river flowing from many sources into a reservoir which, by constant supply, grew ever bigger and dirtier. Islam aims at drying up this river by cutting off its sources, and by dispersing the water in the reservoir by opening up ways of escape.

The Islamic scholar says that Islam did not recognize any of the traditional sources of slavery except that of legal war, that is, war declared by the ruler of the Moslems on the grounds that it is to the benefit of Islam and the Moslem people — war to defend the community from the invader or from those who abrogated their covenants with the Moslems. War is permitted only, however, under the condition that it must be waged in accordance with Islamic teachings. If this condition was not fulfilled, all the captives must be considered free from the beginning.

The "Official" Attitude

But, say the jurists, Islam plans to set free even the prisoners of these legal wars by one or another of the following means:

1. The utterance of the master, made seriously or not seriously, that he freed his slave, even if it was made by mistake.
2. The progeny of female slaves by their masters are free and the mothers are free after the death of the masters and, therefore, there is no right to sell the mother after the birth of the child or even to give her as a present to any other person.
3. It is an acceptable action, in Islam, for the master to free his slave for a time so that he may gain a certain sum which will be given to the master to free him from slavery, and some of the authorities on Islam have stated that it is the right of the slave, too, to ask his master for such an arrangement in accordance with the saying of the Koran — "And such of your slaves as seek a writing [of emancipation] write it for them if you are aware of Good in them."
4. To make an expiation of many sins or wrongdoings in Islam you have to free a slave. This refers to such an act as murder without intention. God says: "It is not for a believer to kill a believer unless it be by mistake. He who has killed a believer by mistake must set free a believing slave." Another such sin is that of oath-breaking, or breaking the fast of Ramadan without acceptable excuse. If one whose duty it is to free a slave has not any slave, he must buy one and set him free. Through this command most slaves would achieve freedom.
5. The ruler of the Moslems is commanded by the Koran itself to allocate a part of the general revenue of his Government for the special purpose of helping slaves who seek to free themselves.
6. The Koran and the traditions are filled with verses which stress that the best way to obtain God's commendation is that they free a slave for His sake only.

As Mr. Ghoraba has explained, in all these provisions it is clearly implied that it is those who have been made prisoners of war that are to be made free. Therefore, it can be said that although Islam admitted slavery in the one form, it aimed undoubtedly to abolish it, and that the means by which this was to be brought about were many and wise.

The Islamic theologian no less than the militarist argues that Moslems must have the right to hold as slaves those enemies taken as prisoners of war; otherwise they would be at a military disadvantage. "If this had not been the case," Mr. Ghoraba says, "and the enemies of Islam had been permitted by their own laws and customs to make slaves of Moslems, while knowing that the Moslems were forbidden by their religion to do the same with them, the whole non-Moslem world would have been encouraged to attack the Moslems. . . . It is the duty of Islam to give fair terms in warfare to the Moslems and not to make them weak. . . . The blame for the persistence of slavery lies with those enemies who attack Islam and not with Islam itself."

Mr. Ghoraba, like so many other Islamic savants who seek to explain the Arab institution of slavery, quotes the ideal and ignores the facts. For instance, the theologians will never answer the question, "Why did slavery flourish for *thirteen hundred years* after Mohammad?"

Other more wordly Moslem speakers are less defensive. The Sudanese ambassador, lecturing in London,[2] began in this way: "Islam was the first religion which was seriously concerned with the problem of slavery and tried to restore to slaves their human rights and dignity and which dealt a death blow to the very roots of this cruel institution. . . . All people are born free and should remain free. . . . The laws of Islam regulated the possession of slaves with great equality and justice, then took the practical course in dealing with the whole institution by drying up all its sources and stopping any new inflow of slaves. . . . It is a question of history and facts. . . . No Moslem was allowed to take any more slaves. . . . Slavery became a very unpopular and discredited institution."

It should be noted that the ambassador was speaking to the world's best informed audience on slavery. He concluded his address by telling the Anti-Slavery Society that it should not involve itself in propaganda or political complications. The vote of thanks was moved by Sir Stewart Gore-Browne, who said, ". . . . I speak for myself and many others when I say a great deal of what we have learned was news to us . . . and even at an advanced age such as mine one can broaden one's view and extend one's knowledge."

The historic truth, in the hands of scholars, is somewhat different from the view of the apologists. Professor R. Brunschvig, editor of the *Encylopaedia of Islam,* writes, "Islam, like its two parent monotheisms, Judaism and Christianity, has never preached the abolition of slavery as a doctrine but it has followed their example, although in a very different fashion, in endeavouring to moderate the institution and mitigate its legal and moral aspects. . . . It was only under an overwhelming foreign influence that Islam began, about a hundred years ago, an evolution in doctrine and practice towards the total suppression of slavery, its abolition in law and custom."

As if to emphasize the institutional character of slavery in Islam, Brunschvig points out that the Koran stipulates that the slave has obligations. He is to give loyal service, he is the "shepherd of his master's wealth" and will be asked for an account of it in the next world. His reward in paradise will be twofold if, in addition to performing the usual religious obligations, he has the special merit of having given good advice to his master.

Like other objective scholars, Brunschvig recognizes the great gulf between the ideal and the actual. He concedes that for the majority of Islamic jurists the presumption is in favor of freedom but argues that no adequately

---

[2] To the Anti-Slavery Society, July 29, 1957.

The "Official" Attitude

clear system of sanctions has been evolved to suppress the kidnapping or sale of free people, Moslem or non-Moslem. "Still less do we see any positive denunciation of the practice of castrating young slaves, although it was condemned in principle."

Other scholars of great repute are no less explicit. Professor A.G.B. Fisher and Dr. H.J. Fisher in a scholarly study,[3] point out that many Islamic legal texts make numerous references to commercial regulations relating to slaves and that "religious law provides considerable precedent for regarding slaves in . . . almost a fiscal way." The Fishers note that on some pilgrimages "slaves might be used as a form of travellers' cheques, to help finance the trip."

Two other important misconceptions — or mis-statements — might well be clarified here with the help of the Fishers in their important work.

It is sometimes stated that Moslem law requires the freeing of slaves on the master's death. In fact, this is legally required only in the case of a slave who is *umm-al-walad* (mother of the child) that is, a slave who has borne her master a child. A special category of slave-to-be-freed is a *mudabbar* slave — one who has received his master's assurance that, on the master's death, the slave will be freed. In Moslem law, a *mudabbar* slave may not be sold but he continues to work for his master and his property belongs to his master. A master, too, may still have sexual relations with a female slave who is a *mudabbar*. But, as always, certain qualifications exist. A man may retract his last testament, including the provision to free a slave, and a debtor whose estate does not cover his debts may not legally free a slave. Nor may a slave be made *mudabbar* unless he falls within that third of the estate over which a testator has complete powers of independent allocation.

Further, it was always a fallacy that Moslem did not enslave Moslem, and much evidence disproves it. Baba of Karo, a Hausa women who in 1949 – 50, at the age of 60, told her life story,[4] recalled the days when "there was always fear; war, war, war — they caught a man and they made him a slave, or else they killed him." She remembered that before the British came and "the world was settled" even Moslem clerics dared not travel freely because they would be kidnapped and sold in the market. Moslems had no assured protection against the risk of being caught in the slavery net. Similar memories are commonplace. In Ibadan the story is told of the teacher Malam Harun who set out for Mecca with some of his students; the party was broken up by a slave gang near Lake Chad, some of the students being killed and their teacher falling into slavery.[5]

---

[3] *Slavery and Muslim Society in Africa.*
[4] To Mary Smith; *Baba of Karo,* London, 1954.
[5] O. el-Nager, *West Africa and the Moslem Pilgrimage.* (University of London thesis, 1969).

One major difficulty — for Moslem jurists as much as for Western scholars — is the sheer complexity of laws and traditions relating to slaves, which in any case vary from group to group. For instance the Malikis hold that emancipation is compulsory when the master carries his ill-treatment of his slave to the point of mutilation or disfigurement; the Hanbalis assert that the slave is no more qualified to hold a position of religious magistrature than an official position of secular authority; the Hanafis set themselves apart from the other schools in not permitting the married male slave to use the device of "cursing" instituted by the Koran (Sure xxiv, 6–9), to the advantage of the husband who may accuse his wife of adultery with no legal proof. The hundreds of qualifications, modifications and exceptions to rules further complicate the legislation regarding slaves.

Brunschvig says, ". . . . Wildly discriminatory is the slavery which still obtains today in the desert; in the Sahara on the one hand, in Arabia on the other, for the benefit of the nomad tribes. Tuareg society, divided into three rigid caste groups, used to keep on the lowest level, beneath the nobles and their vassals, the slave groups enfranchised or not, almost all of them black, who were utilised by the dominant class either as tillers of the soil or as servants to men and beasts. Among the beduin of the Arab peninsula and its fringes black slaves may intermarry and acquire property, but however intimate they may be with the master and his family, however great the advantages custom permits them to enjoy, they are never regarded as equals, even after enfranchisement; they are *abid* and *abid* they remain; and marriage with the sons and daughters of them is considered a come-down, by the lowliest of whites."[6]

Islam's claim that it did not perpetuate slavery cannot be seriously entertained. The whole mass of its own official literature concerning slavery establishes the basic fact that slavery was profoundly important to the Islamic way of life and proves, to an extent that nothing else can, that Islam did, and still does, perpetuate the institution. But there is a still more significant fact — that the "great" period of slave *trading* took place *after* the eradication of the slave trading by the Christian nations.

King Ibn Saud, the leading Islamic ruler, told a Western interviewer in the 1940s that he kept slaves as a matter of "divine right," a right he shared with any Moslem Arab able to afford to buy slaves, since the Arabs were the chosen people of God; all others, therefore, were subservient to them.

This attitude would explain the part played by the pilgrimage in the slave trade. The Slavery Commission of the League of Nations stated in their report (a.19,1925, VI, para 44) that the Commission "is informed on authority which it regards as entirely trustworthy that many slaves of foreign origin in the Hijaz [Saudi Arabia] are either young girls who come as

---

[6]*Encyclopaedia of Islam*.

pilgrims or are smuggled for sale, or are persons coming from various countries, accompanying their parents or masters in the pilgrimage to Mecca.'' In 1932 the League's Committee of Experts on Slavery reported that "Pilgrimages to the Holy Places of Arabia are said to provide the principal opportunity for this traffic [enslavement].''

That the holy pilgrimage has been used as a means to promote slavery would appear to be the most conclusive evidence that Islam's attitude to slavery is at least one of toleration if not of approval, a conclusion supported by the *Encyclopaedia of Islam* — "The Wahhabis of Arabia, those uncompromising restorers of the sunna [word] of the Prophet . . . have vigorously maintained their downright antagonism towards abolition. . . . The fact, amplified in the Koran, that slavery is in principle lawful, satisfies religious scruples. . . . Many Moslems would consider total abolition not only undesirable but reprehensible and contrary to the injunctions of the holy Book.''

VIII
The Slavery of Arab Women

> The uncle maded love to his niece and was forced by his brother — her father — to kill her by poison.
>
> *Al-Akhbar,* Cairo, May 10, 1972.

The position of Arab women in Arab society makes them little more than slaves. They are not slaves within any precise legalistic meaning, because we are here discussing Arab and mostly Moslem women, not foreigners, but in the philosophical, speculative and metaphorical sense — and in practice — Moslem women are no less slaves than those foreign women bought for the harem or for labor of one kind or another.

Evidence for this assertion is best taken from contemporary Arab sources, which have multiplied since about 1960, as an increasing number of Arab writers, teachers and doctors, influenced perhaps by experience in Western countries, protest against the injustices and cruelties they see inflcted on Arab women. Some consider that the lot of an Arab woman is much worse than that of a slave.

This is certainly so in the use of excision or clitoridectomy — the removal of the clitoris or genital organ of a woman — for many Arab women have sufered this abuse, but few slaves. The purpose is to "safeguard" the woman's chastity by removing the means of sexual satisfaction. This feminine "circumcision" to ensure fidelity has had direct consequences on slavery. The Moslem husband, having taken up to four wives, finds all of them "frigid" and incapable of replying to his attentions (because of the operation); so for pleasure he has physical relationships with slave women.

The Arab male's obsession with chastity puts every woman in a position of great danger and tension in case she does something "wrong." An Arab sociologist, Youssef el Masri, in a scholarly work,[1] has listed many examples of the result of *ird* — the sense of family honor — imposed on women.

He quotes the case of Mohammed Abdul Mahmoud who, on July 13, 1959, entered the police station at Gamalieh, Cairo, holding a knife dripping with blood. Applauded by a large crowd, he admitted that he had just killed his sister, aged 16, because he had noticed that she often met a young man in the street. Mahmoud was not punished, since he had acted by right and custom. "This obsession with virginity reaches the limit of horror and absurdity," el Masri wrote, and related the case of Khalaf Moustapha who, in July 1962, outside the office of the provincial attorney in Assuit, Upper Egypt, cut off the head of his 12-year-old niece. *In his view she was guilty of having been raped.* He was expressing the tradition that every woman belongs to the men of the family and that any infringement of her honor is an insult to the honor of her father, her husband, brother, son or uncle, any one of whom may exact *ird*. But punishment is principally directed against the woman. This is most clearly and tragically shown in the punishment inflicted on women considered guilty of adultery, especially in those countries which rigidly invoke the letter of the religious law. In Saudi Arabia the guilty woman — since no trial takes place, she is presumed guilty rather than found guilty — is stoned to death. A European doctor has described such an execution.

> A woman who had been taken in adultery had all her clothes torn off and was dragged at the end of a rope naked through the town. There she was buried with only her head sticking out. A cart full of stones drove up and the many spectators armed themselves. They took up positions in a circle around the victim and at a signal from a police officer they stoned the helpless woman. The bombardment of her head went on until only a bleeding mass remained. So they extended the grave a little. The woman's lover was given fifty lashes and released.[2]

One of the most authoritative and objective writers on the subject of the abuse of Arab women is Dr. Nawal al-Sa'dawi, an Egyptian, who published *Women and Sex* in 1972.[3] Some of Dr. Sa'dawi's experiences are presented here, mostly in the first person.

Worse than Slavery

We know historically how masters acquired slaves. For slaves were

---

[1] *Sexual Drama of Women in the Arab Orient.* (Paris: Laffont, 1962); since translated into nine languages.
[2] Jorgen Bisch. *Behind the Veil of Arabia.*
[3] The Arab Institute for Studies and Publications. The translations used here are by Dr. B. M. Damon.

bought and sold for money, and when a master bought a slave, this slave became a servant to the master without pay. A slave could not leave the service of his master unless the master released him, or sold him in the slave market to a new master. The slave's duty was absolute obedience and the master had the absolute right to do with his slave as he saw fit, with no account due to anyone; for example, extracting his testicles with a scalpel, so that the slave was deprived of his manhood [though he may still be capable of intercourse: Author] and thus could be in attendance on the master's women without giving reason for apprehension.

The acquisition of a woman by a man as his property does not greatly differ from the acquisition of a slave by a master. For a woman is expropriated by means of a down-payment paid to her guardian, usually her father or her older brother. The first article of the marriage contract stipulates that a wife is the property of her husband to whom she owes absolute obedience and must serve in his house without pay. In case she disobeys her husband or complains, or becomes sick, or weak — her husband has the right to divorce her.

The text of Article 67 of the Marriage Law in our [Egyptian] society states:

"No alimony is due to a wife if she refused to surrender herself [sexually] to her husband, without right, or if she was compelled to do so for any reason unrelated to her husband. Likewise, no alimony is due her in case she is imprisoned, even if unjustly, or arrested, or raped, or left her husband's house, or was forbidden by her guardian from maintaining sexual relations with her husband, or she was in any condition which rendered her useless as a wife."

There is no doubt that this text is a clear indication of the kind of relationship between husband and wife, akin to that of master and slave. Nay, for the slave had, under tradition, to be treated if he became sick, and the master had to bear the expense of that treatment, while the wife is denied that right. So if she becomes ill and cannot respond to the sexual desires of her husband, he has the right to throw her out of his house and to deny her alimony, leaving her no choice but to roam the streets, beg, or resort to prostitution. Moreover, if she were to be imprisoned, even though unjustly, or were to be assaulted or raped by some man, her husband has also the right to expel her and to deprive her of her alimony.

By the same token, if the wife spent her youth serving as a maid to her husband and children, but afterwards she became worn out or exhausted or sick, or in any other way unable to fulfill all her obligations and suffers any condition that renders her "useless" as a wife, her husband has the right to spit her out as one spits out a kernel.

The expression "being useless as a wife" denotes that the marital relationship is in essence based on the use of a woman by the man and his ugly exploitation of her self, uglier than the exploitation of the serf by the landowner, or the slave by the master, who used, at least, to be embarrassed if he were to sell his slave while the latter was ill; while a wife, if she becomes sick — by the force of law — must return to her family so that they can treat her because her husband is not responsible for doing that.

On the other hand, the expression "surrender herself" indicates the kind of relationship between husband and wife: The woman is the one who surrenders herself and the man is the recipient of that self as if that "self" were a piece of commercial goods.

Moreover, when a wife is divorced, with or without reason, her price depreciates on the marriage market, exactly like any other used piece of goods.

Honor is Opposed to Slavery

She was a young woman of thirty, when she came to my clinic complaining of aches and inflammation in her womb. I asked about her background and learned that her father was a government clerk and that one day he was approached by a widower of fifty-five, a wealthy cloth merchant and landowner, who asked to marry his daughter. Although she was only eighteen at the time, the father gave his consent without hesitation. Thus, this girl came to live twelve long years with a decrepit old man, who was, at the same time, her husband — and a complete stranger. She had no children by him. Sexual relations between the two had always occasioned in her a strange mental condition which began with a feeling of extreme repulsion and ended with an inexplicable case of pain in the womb and general nausea.

She said sadly: "Every night, I used to feel that I was selling my body, like a prostitute, to this old man, a stranger, in exchange for the few Egyptian pounds he had paid my father."

Is it at all possible to call such a relationship between a wife and her husband honorable? Is it honorable for a father to sell his daughter as a commodity in the name of the marriage institution? Is it honorable for a man to buy for himself a wife who is young enough to be his granddaughter? Is it honorable to force a young girl to live out her life against her free will and against her human nature, while deprived of any enjoyment or right, including the right of motherhood?

A marriage contract, then, is not that which makes a relationship between man and wife honorable. Signing a contract does not suffice to make a man honorable. Buying and selling a woman like merchandise in the name of matrimony is a kind of prostitution concealed beneath a mask of false legality which negates the very essence of honor and its most elementary meaning. For honor, in essence, negates falsehood and forgery, and stands against the acquisition or exploitation of one human being by another. Honor, at root, is opposed to slavery and bondage. It calls for the dignity of man and established relations between human beings on a foundation of love, mutual will and free choice. Honor is predicated on not treating people like commodities, whether they be slaves or women. Consequently, honor is against marriage based on trade and the sale of women for money. Honor, essentially, forbids such a marriage and deems it illegal because it would constitute a relation that negates the honor of man, his dignity, free will, and the freedom of choice that stems from true and sincere feeling. . . .

The Virgin Who Really Was

I still remember that girl, although ten years or more have passed since I saw her. I was then a young M.D., having established my clinic on Giza Square. At that time I was thinking of closing the clinic, for I was convinced, after spending fifteen years in studying medicine and in practicing it, both in Egypt and outside, that most of the patients were not sick but rather were driven by their adverse social conditions to feel chronically ill.

On that day I was sitting and deliberating whether or not to close the clinic when this girl entered my office. I was appalled by her strange and terrified look, as if seeking desperately for help. Years have passed since then and I have forgotten entirely the girl's features — but that look remains engraved in my memory. It became a part of me.

She was not alone. A man accompanied her and he said in a harsh, agitated voice: "Examine her, Doctor, please!"

I addressed my question to the girl: "What do you complain of?" But the girl remained silent, giving no answer to my question.

The man said with a voice harsher and more agitated: "We were married yesterday and I discovered she was not a virgin!"

I asked: "And how did you discover that?"

He answered angrily: "That is obvious; I did not find red blood!"

The girl tried to open her mouth to say something but he stopped her. "She claims she is innocent. I want you to examine her."

I found out, after examining her, that the girl had a hymen and it was completely intact, of the type medically termed as "elastic," because it expands and contracts without tearing and without passing even one drop of blood.

I explained the matter precisely to the husband, who was an educated man who had done his studies abroad. I supposed that he understood and that I had convinced him. The bride's chest heaved with a sigh, as though she breathed for the first time after a long strangulation.

However, the affair did not end with such simplicity. A few days later the girl came back alone. Her face had ceased to be the face of the eighteen-year-old girl whom I had seen a few days before, but was that of a woman who has aged prematurely. Pain and distress showed on her face in an expression akin to that on corpses. She told me with a catch in her voice: "He divorced me. It would have been a disastrous scandal, had not my father kept things quiet."

I asked her: "But didn't your father understand?"

She shook her head. Her withered eyes betrayed tears that flowed and dried, flowed and dried, until they could flow no more. She said: "Nobody believes I am innocent except you, Doctor. I now live in terror lest my father or brother avenge their honor by killing me."

So I went with her to her father and explained the matter to him. I told him that his daughter was a virgin and that her hymen was of the elastic kind that would not tear except upon the birth of her first baby. The father was startled when he heard this scientific fact and he began to beat his palms against each other — a gesture of indignation and perplexity. Then he said angrily: "My daughter has been abused, then!"

"Yes," I said.

"And who is responsible for that?"

I said: "You are — her husband and her family."

I decided then to go back to my office and write something on the subject, but it seemed to be that treatment was needed in several areas. It was not just a medical case, but a social, economic and ethical matter of which medicine constituted only one aspect.

Years passed and I witnessed other stories of different problems: innumerable tragedies of young girls, women and children, who fell victims to prevailing ignorance and tradition. Some of them actually died during abortion, female circumcision or in childbirth under bad conditions; or were murdered because virginity could not be established. Some of these women died a psychological and social death as a result of a tragedy, or for some other reason. And many are the reasons in a society which exposes women to psychological death, to live out their lives in a state more like death. Death would have been a more merciful thing in many cases . . . .

A peasant girl, about sixteen, came to my clinic with her husband. She was pale and emaciated, giving the impression that she was a child of twelve, for her body was unusually small. I supposed that her under-developed body was the outcome of malnutrition, though her pallor made me suspect that she had blood-poisoning. However, when she took off her wide peasant dress, I noticed her bulging belly. Her husband informed me that he had married her one year before, that she had begun to complain of stomach-ache, and that he thought she was pregnant. In her fifth or sixth month.

I asked her the customary question: "When did menstruation cease with you?"

She answered that she had never had any menstrual blood, while her husband commented that she was too young and had not yet reached puberty. He thought that pregnancy was the reason for the absence of menstruation.

When I examined the girl, I found out that there was no fetus in her womb, six months old or five! All that was there was a mysterious swelling. Of course I proceeded to examine the womb by way of the vagina, and there I discovered something which surprised me: the vagina was hermetically blocked by a thick and elastic membrane which I could press with my finger and reach almost as deep as her womb without tearing it.

I asked the husband if he remembered what happened on the first night of their marriage. Promptly he answered: "I had sexual intercourse with my wife but there was no blood. However, I did not suspect her because she was still very young and had not reached puberty yet."

I told the husband that his wife was still a virgin, having been born with a thick and closed hymen and that this swelling of her belly was the menstrual blood which had accumulated month after month, without finding an outlet for itself.

I then opened the membrane with a scalpel and the old accumulated blood flowed out. The girl left the couch as if she had opened her eyes for the first time after a chronic illness or long-term blood poisoning.

I had once read about a murder case which resembled this case. The police discovered the body of a pregnant girl murdered for reasons connected with defense of honor, but the post-mortem examination showed that the swelling of the girl's belly was not caused by pregnancy but by the accumulation of menstrual blood resulting from a thick and closed hymen.

The Dearest Thing in a Woman's Life

A girl of eighteen came with her father to see me. The story was that the girl was an athlete who rode horses and bicycles. Her father had by chance read in a journal that some sports like bicycle or horseback riding, or jumping down from high places might rupture the hymen. Since that time he had been worried, and had forbidden his daughter to engage in her favorite sports. He wanted now to be reassured as to the "safety" of her hymen before he gave her in marriage to her cousin.

I then asked the girl about the kind of sports she had engaged in and whether she recalled a specific incident which caused her to feel pain or to observe drops of blood. The girl answered in the negative, stating that she had not had any accident and that her father's worries were exaggerated to the point of forbidding her to engage in sports which she loved as she loved life. She said with some sadness: "If marriage means that I cannot engage in sports, then I do not want to marry. I prefer sports to marriage."

I believed completely in the right of the girl to engage in sports and therefore advised the father to forget his worries and let his daughter enjoy her sports. But the father was not convinced, and he insisted that I examine her.

Upon examination I found that the daughter's hymen was of the ordinary type with a regular circular opening. However there was, at one side of the opening, a rupture two or three millimetres long caused by the violent sport in which she engaged. I explained the matter to the father whose anxiety and worry multiplied. He asked whether this small tear was a loss of virginity and whether there would be "no blood" on the wedding night. I told him the truth, that such a rupture has naturally enlarged the opening of the membrane and that there might be "no blood" on the wedding night, especially if she happened to marry a man whose sexual organ was smaller in size than usual.

Then the father's anxiety reached a greater height and he began to tremble and ask in perplexity: "And so what is there to do, Doctor?"

I said: "Nothing. You have only to explain the matter to the man who will marry your daughter."

The father said in great consternation: "This is the greatest tragedy that has occurred in my life!"

I said: "What is the tragedy? Did your daughter lose an arm or a leg or one of her eyes?"

He answered: "Had she lost an eye, it would have been easier, but she has lost the dearest thing she has."

I tried to make things easier for him. I said that the dearest thing his daughter possessed was not that membrane that was ruptured without her knowledge or feeling while engaged in her sport, but the same dearest thing any human being has — her free will, her integrity, her participation in the building of a better life for herself and her society.

But he said, "And who will believe that it was because of her engaging in sport? Everybody will suspect her behavior and her honor . . . ."

The father was on the verge of a breakdown. He asked me to sign a medical certificate verifying that the rupture had occurred because of his daughter's engaging in sports and not for any other reasons. I gave him the certificate to calm him down, and he held it in both hands with care and apprehension, as if he held his own life. He then took his daughter by the hand and left.

Will That Affect Her Virginity?

A girl of twenty went to see Dr. Sa'dawi with her mother, an educational inspector in an elementary school in Cairo. The mother asked him to examine her daughter and to reassure her about the "safety" of her hymen. Sa'dawi asked the mother why she doubted her daughter's virginity. She had discovered that her daughter, when washing every morning, put her finger to her hymen to feel and size up its opening. The mother was afraid that her daughter had, in this way, inadvertently damaged her membrane.

The girl explained that her mother warned her continuously of the dangers of jumping or rope-skipping lest she tear her hymen, but she enjoyed the exercise and engaged in it at school. Still, her mother's warnings had caused her much worry; so one day, her anxiety at a peak, while taking a bath she inserted her hand to make sure her hymen was there. When she found with the tip of her finger its small aperture, she was terrified because she thought it was torn. A girl friend told her that all hymens had a small aperture for letting out the menstrual blood and since then the girl used to feel this aperture to reassure herself that it had remained narrow and did not enlarge as a result of her physical activity.

Sa'dawi examined the girl and found out that the membrane was intact except for its aperture, which was enlarged, not because of rope-skipping but because of the repeated insertion of her finger.

The mother asked in terror: "WILL THAT AFFECT HER VIRGINITY?"

Sa'dawi told the mother the truth: if her daughter married, there might not be any blood as a result of her first sexual intercourse.

The mother almost collapsed; so the doctor tried to reassure her by giving her a certificate "absolving" her daughter.

Sa'dawi wrote: The daughter was indeed innocent, for the real guilty party was the mother, who had given her daughter a faulty education and had infused fear and anxiety in her. Perhaps the mother was also innocent because of her ignorance of the facts, and the real culprit was this society which measures its honor by the flimsy membrane, exposed as it is to injury, sagging, scratches and tears. We can imagine the great mental damage inflicted upon young girls in our society when they realize that there is at the end of their vagina a thin membgane considered to be the dearest thing they possess. On it depends their future, their honor and their life. They have to guard it with all means, even if they must stop exercising or if they must walk with mincing steps, accumulating fat in their slow lazy bodies and false conceptions in their minds, living in perpetual fear for their hymen, losing all elements of a strong body and soul, reduced to a life insipid, stale and motionless under the shadow of a husband to whom they had proven their honor on the wedding night by a few drops of blood, and to whom they must continue to prove it every night by their ignorance of, or refraining from every indication of enjoyment which might prove their awareness of what is called sex.

Artificial Defloration

She came to me five months pregnant, but when I proceeded to examine her through the vagina, she jumped, startled, explaining to me that she was still a virgin. She told me her story: She was a student at the university where she had met a boy-friend who loved her. She also loved him, but they never thought about marriage because he had failed in his studies and she was uncertain of his future. Nevertheless, they used to meet and engage in superficial sex acts, harmless to the "integrity" of the hymen. In fact, I discovered that the hymen was intact, though one sperm had succeeded in penetrating her womb through the hymenal aperture, which, as mentioned, had remained intact. In this way, she bore a fetus in her womb, while still retaining her virginity.

The young girl asked me to get rid of her child by performing a Caesarian section operation, so that she might preserve her virginity. But I excused myself from performing such an operation on her; so she left. Then I met her a few years later and she informed me that she had gone to another physician who had consented to perform the operation, and that she had later married a successful engineer and had given birth to two children.

I pictured this successful engineer on his wedding night going through the traditional motions and check-ups to make sure of his bride's virginity, and feeling extremely happy upon finding her hymen intact, caring little for that long, deep incision on her belly. Nay, not even caring a bit if he found an incision on her heart or liver or brain, caring only for an incision in her hymen, even though this incision would have been only one millimetre long — for this would have been the greatest tragedy!

I do not believe that our society ignores the fact that there exist artificial means to restore the semblance of virginity to a girl who has lost it for one reason or another, and that the blood which flows on the wedding night might not always necessarily be that of the bride. It may be chicken blood placed in a small sac, or even menstrual blood because the wedding night had been chosen to coincide with the girl's monthly period, or any other such trick in which "nurses" or those experienced with men and life excel.

How many stories I have heard and cases I have witnessed with my own eyes when I used to practice medicine in the countryside! For a strange marriage tradition still prevails in some of our villages, where the "nurse" comes and seizes the bride by her legs, like holding a chicken before slaughter, then extends her finger, whose long nail is sharpened like a knife — often the nail is grown for the occasion — and with this finger the "nurse" tears the bride's hymen, wiping off the flowing blood with a white "towel" which the bride's father snatches to raise high for all people to see and thereby become eye witnesses to his honor and to the honor of his daughter.

I have attended some of these happy occasions and, driven by my curiosity, I have often sat beside the "nurse" to observe her closely while she performs her act. One time the "nurse" thrust her finger violently inside the bride's vagina, but when only a few drops of blood fell, she scratched the vagina wall with her sharpened nail. Blood flowed profusely, soaking the "towel". Triumphant screams and drum-beatings filled the air. I whispered to the "nurse" that she had wounded the vagina, but she whispered back that this was necessary in order to produce more blood, for people measure the bride's honor by the quantity of blood that drops on the towel.

The experienced nurse told me: "When I used to tear only the hymen, only a few drops of blood would fall which the old peasant women, with their long tongues, could not see clearly. Therefore I trained myself to wound the vagina wall with my long nail to cause hemorrhage. I have acquired a good reputation here and all the families insist that I alone, to the exclusion of the other nurses, perform deflorations in wedding festivities."

The majority of physicians who have practiced in Egyptian villages have been witnesses to many painful incidents emanating from this Egyptian custom of defloration by the finger. Sometimes this may be the finger of an experienced "nurse," but at other times it is the finger of the husband. In such cases the damage is more substantial and ugly because it is a coarse, ignorant finger which has previously touched nothing more delicate than a shovel. On such cases the finger is thrust with brutality, coarseness, and blind ignorance inside the girl's small vagina, tearing up the fine tissues, sinking into the flesh and nerves, causing ruptures whose damage could not be cured in a lifetime. I shall never forget that bride who was carried to me in the middle of her wedding night hemorrhaging profusely from her vagina. When I examined her it was evident that she had a gaping hole in her bladder caused by her husband's thick and long finger which had gone through the vagina wall and into the bladder, piercing it and leaving a big hole. . . . Many other physicians can tell you of many similar cases.

The existence of a hymen and the dripping of a few drops of blood are not proof of anything. When these facts become evident to some people, they exclaim in apprehension: "Then how can we judge a woman's honor?" But what do these people understand by "honor"? Is honor merely that a woman protects her sexual organs? Is a girl honorable if she safeguards her hymen, though she does not safeguard her mind, her honesty, her ability to work and produce? Does the girl who tells lies become honorable merely because she was born with a hymen? Is it possible that honor is an anatomical attribute? And if we grant that the hymen is proof of a girl's honor, what then is the proof of a man's honor?

Some people say that a man's honor has no need of proof. Does this mean that in the eyes of society all men are honorable? Others will answer saying that a man's honor differs from that of a woman. "A man is not shamed except if his pocket be empty," says one of our popular proverbs. This means that a man is honorable so long as he works and has money, notwithstanding his sexual relations with women. Nay, a man in our society is proud of his numerous affairs with women and considers that a kind of victory and triumph.

From this we realize that Arab society has two different yardsticks by which it measures honor and that it has imposed sexual virtue on women alone. From this stems the strange social phenomenon that a woman avoids man in order to preserve her honor, while man pursues woman because he desires her and because her pursuit and contact does not shame him in any form or fashion. Thus the man persists in pursuing a girl, using all tricks possible for that purpose. He uses sometimes love and passion, sometimes promises to marry, often also promises of faithfulness forever and manifestations of sincerity, so that when the girl believes and trusts him, society will say about her that she has become a fallen woman. If the man betrays her and does not marry her, society again brands her with dishonor, destroying her future and her child's future, while the man feels free, successful and happy, to repeat his experiences under the very aegis of society.

The following is taken from *Akbar al-Yom*, Cairo, October 12, 1974:

No, no, Miss . . . We Want a Male Engineer.

Durayya Shafiq Nayruz Hanna got her B.Sc. from the Institute for High Industrial Studies in Shabbin al-Kom in Egypt (Electrical Engineering) in May, 1973.

In January 1974 all the graduates of her class got letters of appointment [in the Egyptian Government] except her!

She then inquired at the Personnel Department (of the central government) responsible for her appointment. She was told that she had been appointed at the Ministry of Agriculture.

So she went to the Ministry of Agriculture where she was told that they were looking for a suitable position for her in one of the sections near Shabbin al-Kom where she resided.

She waited two months for a word from the Ministry of Agriculture. Then she was told that she had been appointed in the Meat Divison at Cairo where she had to go to start work.

At the Meat Division she was told that they were indeed in need of an engineer, but they needed a male, not a female one, whereupon she was transferred back to the Ministry of Agriculture and provided with a letter to this effect.

At the Ministry of Agriculture they told her: "Go find another Ministry which will accept your services, and we will be ready to forego our privilege of benefiting from your services."

After long searches in many ministries, the responsible officials in the Ministry of Housing promised her an appointment — but nothing happened. After repeated visits to the Ministry of Housing during a period of two months, she was finally able to get an interview with the General Director of the Ministry. The Director agreed to appoint her in Shabbin al-Kom, and sent a letter to the Ministry of Agriculture asking for a release of her financial allotment in their budget [the reason being that there was no allotment for her position in the Ministry of Housing] or to "lease" her to the Ministry of Housing with her salary paid by the Ministry of Agriculture.

The Ministry of Agriculture refused to release her allotment. It also refused to "lease" her to the Ministry of Housing while paying her salary. She had to find another way.

She succeeded in getting a letter from the General Director of the Ministry of Agriculture addressed to the central Personnel Department, in which he expressed the Ministry's agreement to appoint her anywhere else. The officials in charge at the Personnel Department promised her that they would effect the necessary changes in her status to transfer her to the Ministry of Education and Culture, on condition that she succeed, by her own personal endeavours to get that Ministry to agree to accept her.

For the next two months she did the following: On July 11, 1974, she travelled to the Ministry of Education and Culture in Cairo so that she would be able to follow up the progress of her applications.

On August 3, she obtained the information that her file got as far as the 9th floor on the building of the Majma so she went there. There she was told: "Come back in two days!"

On August 12, they told her that all work on her file was frozen pending the return of the General-Inspector.

On August 17, she obtained the information that her file was in the hands of Mr. Abd al-Nur Bibawi who then left on vacation.

On August 21, they told her:"Do not trouble yourself in vain, your file will remain frozen until the return of the General-Inspector from his vacation at the end of the month . . . for no one else has the authority to make a decision on it."

She had become desperate by now, so she stayed at her home in Shabbin al-Kom feeling extremely dejected and insulted, having incurred all these expenses for travelling to and fro between Shabbin al-Kom and Cairo for eight months without any result whatsoever equal to half the monthly salary of her father, whereas her father was a small clerk whose salary was hardly sufficient to provide for the barest necessities. Her mother was paralysed and bound to the house, and her treatment was stopped because of the deficit in their budget caused by the daughter's travels to Cairo. They endured so much to realize her hopes becaue they had no other child and she was their only hope in life.

Suddenly she got a letter from the Ministry of Agriculture dated August 7, demanding that she proceed immediately to her work, failing which the Ministry would be compelled to bring the matter before the District Attorney! Full of happiness, she immediately headed for the Ministry of Agriculture to start work. There, she was given a letter addressed to the Institute of Agricultural Insurance. She went there in haste to be told that the Director of the Institute was not there, would she come back tomorrow? She had to get back to Shabbin al-Kom in tears; her parents wept with her.

She came back "tomorrow" and "after tomorrow" till in the end she begged them to have pity on her because she could no longer afford the travel expenses. They then told her: "We are sorry, Miss, we have no need of you!"

She went back to the Ministry of Agriculture on foot to save the bus fare trying all the time to hide her tears from the passers-by. The Director of the Personnel Department told her to give him the time so he could find her another job, and "In case we fail, we will tell you good-bye."

On September 10, the Ministry of Education and Culture wrote her a letter expressing their regret for not giving her an appointment because she was "a female."

After all these comedies, we have no comment, leaving the task to the Personnel Department.

There Was No Blood

The Supreme Court of Baghdad heard a case of alleged malpractice attributed to an official government physician. *The Iraqi Medical Journal*, January, 1972, published this report of the case.

> This physician was asked to examine a young girl in order to determine whether she was a virgin or whether she had been deflowered recently or a long time before. The reason leading the judge to ask for this medical examination was that her husband had told her family on the wedding night that he doubted their daughter's virginity since there was no blood as a result of the intercourse. The physician then made the examination, left the room, and when her family insisted that he inform them of the result, he announced that the girl was not a virgin and that she had been deflowered a long time before. The news fell upon them like a bolt of lightning. Her cousin was so angry that he murdered the girl the next day. The post-mortem examination of the body proved, however, that the physician's pronouncement to the family had, in fact, no basis of truth whatsoever and that the girl's hymen was not ruptured at all. The judge formed a committee to examine the girl's body and the committee reported that the hymen was intact and that it was of the elastic type, thus proving the mistaken diagnosis of the government physician.

A Wife Is Mere Chattel

In a study by Dr. Sayyid Uways, adviser to the Egyptian National Centre for Social and Criminal Research, the most important factor confronting birth control in Egyptian society was defined as the low status of women. He gave the following reasons for this low status:

1. Because the Egyptian family is a patriarchal, not a matriarchal one; males take on responsibilty and family descent is related to the father, not the mother.
2. A female is raised to become a "housewife"; therefore her social role outside her family is extremely limited. "A girl's arena is the house" is a popular Egyptian saying.
3. Egyptian females are not allowed to take important jobs which are assigned to males only — in the areas such as the judiciary, legislation, religious leadership, membership in the army or police force.
4. The right of the Egyptian female to vote and run for office is a "right" which must be approved.
5. A woman marries only in order to serve her husband. This service includes all the roles a wife is supposed to play, such as housekeeper, mother to his children and mistress.
6. The further lowered status of the Egyptian female in the situation where her husband takes a second wife.
7. The lowered status of the Egyptian female if she remains unmarried.
8. The Egyptian female's value is subject to market fluctuations so that marriage money paid for her goes up or down according to whether she is a "virgin" or not. If she is a virgin, her price is higher, while if she is a divorcee or a spinster, her price is less. And woe to the female who has passed a suitable marriage age: her price is abysmal.
9. In many cases, the Egyptian female is forced to marry.
10. A wife is, in the eyes of her husband, mere chattel.
11. A wife lives under the roof of her husband and suffers his bad treatment which never changes into mature and wise behaviour. She bears patiently all sorts of complications — his marrying a second wife — and hardships — cursings and beatings — for her piece of bread, or so that she will be protected by a man. "The shadow of a man is preferable to the shadow of a wall" is a popular saying.
12. A wife lives a life of anxiety and fear of the spectre of a second (or third or fourth) wife.
13. The Egyptian female can be divorced if she does not give birth to male children. Sometimes she is divorced for trifles.
14. It is not desirable to address the Egyptian female by name, in case she is a wife or a mother: This would be considered an improper approach as all communication must be through a male of the family.
15. The male child is preferred by the father and the mother.
16. The Egyptian woman, when walking in the street with one male member of the family, has to walk behind him.
17. The term "woman" is a pejorative one, considered an insult or a curse if attributed to a male.
18. The married female has no right to divorce unless this right has been explicitly mentioned in the marriage contract — and that is rare.

19. The Egyptian female is in demand in marriage in accordance with her family's name and status.
20. Egyptian females of a certain age and under certain conditions are forbidden to mix with males.
21. Women are considered to be lacking in intelligence and religion.
22. The percentage of female skilled workers is a very small one.
23. Egyptian female workers, whether skilled or unskilled, work under the domination of the Egyptian male in most cases. Female peasants work but they do so under miserable conditions likewise dominated by males.
24. Females inherit a lesser portion than males.
25. The percentage of illiteracy and analphabetism among females is extremely high, reaching, in some of the Egyptian villages, as high a level as just under 100 per cent.

The Omnipotent Husband

The Iraqi writer, Abd al-Rahman al-Darbandi, interviewed at length the Special Supervisor of the Ministry of Education of the Government of Iraq, Mr. Ahmad al-Sharbati. The interview was published in *The Contemporary Iraqi Woman*[4] and the following is a brief extract.

> O, most virtuous Iraqi woman, heed my advice because it stems from my experience in life:
> Do not imitate others except in that which enhances your behaviour, guards your honour and protects your being.
> Do not accuse your husband of bad taste or bad judgment, because after all he has chosen you from among other women to be his wife.
> Never forget the favour your husband did for you. Never forget what he spends on you and your comfort.
> Never keep any secret from your husband, for he would know it, and he will suspect you.

Force is the Family Bond

Bearing in mind the position in the Moslem family of the male, who is the all-powerful master in his patriarchal environment, it is not surprising that the recommendations of the Koran have been interpreted in a restrictive rather than liberal sense concerning slaves and women. E. F. Gautier writes of the situation as being similar to that of the slave.[5]

> The harem is a small state within the state. Over it the father exercises, by divine grace, a delegation of public power; he is a sovereign there, an absolute sovereign, a sultan. . . . Force being the family bond in Islam, it is atural that the Moslem house is laid out in the way it is. It is a fortress, turning blind

---
[4](Baghdad: Dar Al-Basri Press, 1970).
[5]*Moeurs et Coutumes des Musalmans*. Paris, 1965.

practically windowless walls to the outside world, to the street. In the West, the family can endure, even in the humblest conditions, for centuries, or generations at least. It certainly survives the father because it is built around something other than his authority. The harem, being what it is, yields completely to the authority of the master, man, during his lifetime. It becomes easy to understand another peculiarity of the Eastern family which usually escapes attention; it has no name. There are no family names in the East. There are only first names; everyone has his own and adds to this his father's. The Moslem family is made for the father, for him alone; it is his during his lifetime. Consequently, it disappears with him when he dies; his harem, where his authority was the only bond, is immediately dissolved. Another harem begins, with no connection or continuity with the one which has just disappeared.

Al-Haj Bashir, ruler of Bornu, mentioned in an earlier chapter as a friend of Heinrich Barth, had a harem of perhaps 400. Barth thought he regarded his collection as a kind of ethnological museum, for Bashir made great efforts to acquire a perfect specimen of each tribe; he told Barth proudly that he also possessed a Circassian woman, a rarity in that region. When he specially fancied some woman owned by some notable of his race who refused to sell her, Bashir would order that she be handed over. Bashir was executed in 1853 and, according to Barth, 73 sons survived him; no record, of course, was kept of the number of daughters.

Anguish in Algeria
An English medical student, Ian Young, spent part of the summer of 1970 at an Algerian hospital, for further training in midwifery. Dr. Young later wrote a perceptive, sensitive record of his experiences — *The Private Life of Islam*.[6] It reveals, at times all too vividly in medical detail, the lowly place of women in Algerian society. In the following extract a man has arrived at Young's hospital to collect his wife and sends in his cousin to bring her out.

> I check on the register and remember the girl well. She came in bleeding, but with her cervix still closed. She's resting in bed. The bleeding's stopped, and with a little more rest she should be able to keep the baby. I remember her because of the nasty wound on the inside of her leg — a raw area about four inches by two, very painful and leaking fluid. An old woman had done it up in the village with burning wood, as treatment for her (vaginal) bleeding.
>
> So I tell the cousin that she should stay a little longer. Take her back to the mountains now, and to her daily routine, and she'll almost certainly lose the baby. The cousin goes out to the car and comes back with the husband. . . . He's taking his wife home, he says, there are children for her to look after and

[6](London:Allen Lane, 1970).

a home to keep.... I explain it all again and ask how far he is from the hospital. He's four hours away, he says. Supposing she miscarries, I tell him. By the time he's got her here she could be already dead, especially as she's so weak already. "But there's water to fetch," says the man, "figs to pick, fields to look after, the children...."

Emergency followed emergency and tragedies were commonplace, as Young illustrates in a poignant story about a young bride.

> I hear a fresh set of screams and after I've fought my way through the crowd outside the curettage room door I find him [Dr. Kostov, a colleague] seated between a fresh set of legs. The girl's about sixteen and she's naked. She's running with sweat and sobbing into the elbow crooked about her face.
> It's not a curettage. I become aware of the girl's pink breasts and flat belly. She's not even pregnant. I see the fresh henna on her hands and feet [applied before marriage, as sexually attractive] as Dr. Kostov readjusts the spotlight — she won't stop moving — I notice how carefully she's been shaved. She'd look just like a little girl, if it wasn't all so swollen and sore. Simply to be touched there with cotton wool makes her jump and squirm. It's a marriage injury — a torn hymen, a lacerated vagina — and blood's everywhere. The discarded wedding robe's steeped in it.... The girl lies panting, drawing in hoarse lungfuls of air, energy, further screams. Those men I had to push my way through to get in here, four or five of them, all in fine suits, their best clothes, must have been the marriage party....
> Outside, his finger [Dr. Kostov's] points.... One of the men comes forward. "No love for twenty days," grunts Dr. Kostov. The husband smiles, with an air of complicity. "Come now, Doctor." He's about forty, trim and sophisticated in an English blazer with colours over the breast pocket....
> Dr. Kostov insisted that the girl should stay in the hospital until the bleeding stopped but the husband objected that she had nothing wrong with her. The husband asked Young, with a wink, what was left of a marriage when the bride had to stay in the hospital? He insisted that he would take his wife away even when Kostov said that she would certainly need more treatment.

Young continues:

> The husband takes the handkerchief from his breast pocket to wipe the vomit from the girl's mouth. His mother comes forward and together they lift the girl into a sitting position, swinging her legs over the side of the trolley, first stage of getting her to her feet....
> They took her away from the hospital.

The end of the slavery of Arab women within their own society is in sight, but a long way off. Much depends on education, which so many Arab girls still do not receive — although the Prophet advocated the education of women. But the existence already of an educated female class, small though it is, supplies the basis for progress. Even in the male bastion of Libya a few women are beginning to find places as teachers, journalists and information officers. In Lebanon, the most advanced Arab country, many women are in the professions, but generally they are Christian rather than Moslem. In Saudi Arabia it is still rare for a Moslem girl to have a career, unless she leaves the country. A young Saudi Arabian girl, trained in the United States as a radiologist, told me that in leaving her country she has escaped from slavery. "The Arab male does not want a marriage partner," she said, "but a possession over which he has total ownership. And if you try to convince him that a genuine partnership would be a much better relationship he becomes afraid for his dominance and falls back on religion as evidence for his supreme authority."

A desert Arab — but a traveled one and by his own standards, educated — once told me, "A goat for relief, a boy for pleasure, a woman for breeding — that's the best approach to sex." His attitude is hardly universal in the Arab world, but it does indicate the relative place of women in the minds of many Arab men.

The existence of the eunuch is proof of the Arab obsession with chastity. The eunuch's principal role was to guard the harem, a delicate duty which demanded castration, an operation carried out on such a large number of slaves that the word "Siklabi" (slave) often means eunuch in Arabic, though castration is contrary to the spirit of the Koran. C.W.W. Greenidge, one-time director of the Anti-Slavery Society, considered castration "the most revolting consequence of slavery."

Since wives are forced to live under the husband-master's orders, more out of fear than love, there developed private police forces or "gardiens de femmes," who could only be trusted if they were made sexless. In Arab literature many books concern the eunuch, his role in the family and the technique of castration. It is interesting to note that, in the experience of the Arab slave-merchants, castration often increases the intelligence of white slaves, but tends to diminish the intelligence of Negroes. Various methods of castration have been used in the Arab world. On Negroes it was "a fleur de ventre"(abdomen level) so that they had no use of their penis. This type of castration was applied with such savagery that one is inclined to think that some racial feeling was involved. It has been said that ninety per cent of Negro slaves castrated in this way died from the results of the operation. Lord Cromer wrote in 1908: "The operation is carried out in the most cruel and barbaric way by people who are completely lacking in surgical experience. . . . Most English people are aware of the horrors of slavery. They know how peaceful villages in Central Africa are invaded by bands of Arab ruffians; how the old, men and women alike, are killed pitilessly; how children and girls are brought to the coast and how they die of exhaustion, on the way. This, after the boys have suffered the most terrible process of mutilation imaginable for a man. The very high price paid for these young boys is due to the percentage of deaths during the mutilation."

For the white slaves, in relation to whom the Arabs probably had an inferiority complex, especially the Europeans, other methods of castration were used; some would allow the eunuch to have sexual relations but not to procreate. Many a secret love-affair and many a tragedy took place between the eunuchs and the women they were guarding, since large numbers of these women were sexually unsatisfied.

When the organs were not removed completely, harem orgies could, and did, occur. "The women, knowing that they do not risk being pregnant, try to gain the attention of the young eunuchs," wrote Greenidge. "This is why nowadays many young slaves are made complete eunuchs. . . . It is a horrible operation. . . ."

The horror was partly because of the lack of hygiene and the brutality of the "surgeon." As prices rose, merchants and buyers took more care to safeguard their merchandise. Thus, Arab doctors, or even Europeans or Americans — who maintained that without them the boys would suffer much more — operated in a modern way on the young slaves. Often in the 1950s, the operation was a favor which the doctor of a major petrol company was called upon to do for the powerful princes of Arabia.

The Anti-Slavery Society of London reported a letter dated September 28, 1956, confirming that castration of slaves for harems was taking place by doctors in hospitals, and under anesthesia. The letter also confirmed that in all known cases, castration consisted of a total removal of the genital organs, and was practiced on children of ten to fourteen years of age.

Though the making of eunuchs was said to be strictly forbidden by Mohammad, Moslem rulers have often found eunuchs attractive not only as harem keepers but as senior politicians, since they could not fulfill any temptation to found a rival dynasty. Around 1800, for instance, the Prince of Muscat, worried that his African dependencies might become too independent, appointed eunuchs as his representatives there, dividing civil and military power between them.

Eunuchs are also employed for religious reasons in mosques. Sometimes it happens that women must be chased from the mosque in Mecca, and as a Moslem is supposed not to touch any women other than his wife or those in his family, eunuchs must do this important task, being neither men nor women. The eunuchs of the Grand Mosque in Mecca wear enormous green turbans, and are called the "aghas." A considerable number, all Negroes, are always on guard.

Sean O'Callaghan saw some of these African future mosque and harem eunuchs as children at a market in Jibouti. "The Somali woman took us into another room where these things [the inspection of girls by Arab merchants] took place. The young boys were in a circle on a platform, their backs to us. They were completely naked, and I noted with horror that five of them were castrated. This time the examination of their posteriors was much more complete [than in the case of the girls]. I noted that the eunuchs had had their organs removed totally. My Somali companion told me later that about ten out of every 100 of the children are castrated; they are sold to homosexual Arabs or else as guards for harems in the Yemen. After an examination with a stethoscope, one of them was immediately eliminated; he was probably suffering from tuberculosis. After the examination, the children aged between ten and twelve years were taken away, all sobbing and crying."[7]

Any writer would be tempted to refer to eunuchs in the past tense, but many exist and some travelers insist that they are still being "produced." No clear evidence exists of this, but the position of the eunuch is inextricably woven with that of women, whether they are Moslem-Arab, paid harem volunteers or slave women. As long as some Arab males have a harem to guard — for the *institution* remains current even if the *term* is obsolescent — eunuchs will be needed to guard it.

[7]*Traffic in Men*, London, 1962.

EPILOGUE

EPILOGUE

As has been seen, for centuries the wealthy Arabs and many poorer ones owned foreign slaves, and their possession caused great satisfaction. The mere thought of a life without slaves would have been intolerable, for they fulfilled basic Arab psychological needs. The gradual decline of the slave trade coincided with the rise of the oil industry, which tended to replace the great void left in the soul of the Islamic world by the "ending" of slavery.

In the mid-1970s the Arab oil-owning states enslaved much of the industrialized world with a new form of bondage — soaring oil prices coupled with the threat to stop supplies altogether if the industrial nations did not acquiesce in certain political demands. To claim that Islam and the Arabs deliberately created a new type of slavery to replace the old would be both to overstate the case and to oversimplify it. But there does exist in Arabs the need to dominate a subservient class; with the gradual disappearance of the menial slave class the oil-desperate Western races partly supplied that need, at least vicariously. Deep and strong motives may be at work, as hinted by an Algerian diplomat who told me, "The West forced Islam to give up its slaves; do you suppose that Islam will forget and forgive that?"

But the West, and the industrialized world at large, is so preoccupied with its own problems that it has not even seen the difficulties suffered by Black Africa and its relationship with the oil-supplying Arab states. During the June, 1974, conference of the Organization of African Unity held in Mogadishu, African delegates, led by Ghana and Ethiopia, criticized the Arab oil producers' refusal to treat OAU African countries as a special case by allowing them a price reduction. Kenya, Zaire, Tanzania, Ethiopia, Ghana and Madagascar described in detail the difficulties and economic hardships which resulted from Arab oil policy. In effect, the conference turned into a tribunal arraigning the Arabs for not fulfilling their promises of help. African newspapers were even more extreme in expressing anti-Arab sentiment. These strong feelings, brought to the surface by the oil issue, are a manifestation of the deep-rooted historical resentment which many Africans feel towards the Arabs.

The slave trade has certainly influenced Black African attitudes towards Arabs, attitudes which find expression even in scholarly works. The Ghanaian scholar, Professor L.H. Ofosu-Appiah, Director of the *Encyclopaedia Africana* Secretariat, comments in a study of slavery:

> On the eastern coast of Africa and in the Sudan the Arab raiders started enslaving Negroes during the period of Islam's empire building. The difference between the methods of the Arabs and those of the European traders was that the Arabs actually went on slave-raiding expeditions and herded slaves to the coast. . . . They travelled as far as the Congo forests and settled around the Great Lakes — Victoria, Nyanza, Tanganyika. Wherever they went they burned down villages and carried off human beings to cart their ivory to the coast. For years the Arabs dominated this area of Africa, and, with the Portuguese, were the only slaving nations which settled in Africa and depopulated it.

Professor Appiah was sure that the slave trade still affected Afro-Arab relations:

> When Arab leaders cannot understand the hostility of some Africans to their regimes, it may be worth reminding them that their part in enslaving Africans is a festering sore which cannot be easily cured.

African newspapers are quick to comment on any news which suggests a revival of the slave trade. The *Weekly Spectator* of Ghana not infrequently runs editorials on the theme, and on February 17, 1973, wrote:

> . . . . Over the past two decades Ghana has led the quest for restoration of the black man's lost glory and set the pace for the rediscovery of the African personality. It is therefore revolting and bewildering to note that [Ghana] is being used for revival of the slave trade. . . . We recall vividly the uncertain days of the struggle for independence when Lebanese and Syrian merchants in Ghana constituted themselves into a volunteer force and with batons cudgelled down freedom fighters in the streets of Accra in open daylight. . . . It appears that we have taken our tolerance too far and they have taken our leniency for weakness and are now adding insult to injury by trading our young daughters like apples or any other commodity. . . . Our children must be defended against slavery.

Epilogue 111

The dislike of Lebanese and Syrian traders common to several African countries contributes to anti-Arab irritation.

Some Arab leaders themselves invoke memories of the slave trade, as did President Qadhafi of Libya when he called for a holy war against Christianity in Africa. The Black African Archbishop of Abidjan, Ivory Coast, writing in the Milan paper, *Avenire* (June 19, 1974), wondered if this would mean a return to the days when 80,000 Africans a year were enslaved by "Arab colonialists."

Black Africans staying in Arab countries as students or visitors encounter discrimination and contempt, an inevitable result of centuries of Arab superiority. One result is that many African editors have asked why the Arabs should be allowed to join the Organization of African Unity when their interests are not in Africa. "The Arabs have their Arab League and if the OAU is to achieve unity the question of the Arab World in African affairs must be settled first."[1]

The fear of Africans about Arab religious, political and economic encroachment is sometimes profound. This is well illustrated by an article in the *Kenya Mirror* (May, 1974).

> After the departure of white colonial rule, the onslaught of the Arabized version of Islam in Black Africa is making inroads with predictable penetration. A new form of colonialism, this time thinly disguised and even more devastating in its impact than the neo-colonialism of which Nkrumah [of Ghana] had warned us so often is enveloping black Africans. The winds blowing across the Sahara do not bring blessing and rain to black Africa. These are the winds of destruction and herald altogether new ominous signs of anxiety and worry.

The practice of identifying the Islamic world with the Arab world — so strongly advocated by President Nasser and several other Arab leaders — is reflected in maps published by the Arab League, which show parts of Eritrea and Niger and the whole of Chad, Senegal, Mali and Mauritania as Arab. The assumption of joint origins and politics angers many Africans, but African politicians cannot always reveal their anger. They are torn between the survival-need to remain friendly with the Arab oil states and the desire to keep themselves from being drawn into Arab politics. Nigeria, with its own oil, can be more outspoken than others. "The Middle East war is an Arab and not an Islamic war, so that Moslems of Nigeria should avoid taking an unfair stand in the Middle East problem."[2]

Traditional arguments are frequently used by African commentators.

---

[1] *Daily News*, Zambia, June 21, 1974.
[2] *Daily Times*, Nigeria, September 9, 1969.

"Military Pan-Arabism is essentially racist and is therefore bound to favour slavery. It should not appeal to black Africans."[3]

In African minds, imperialism is almost synonymous with slavery, and the fear that the first will bring the second finds expression almost daily.

> The Arab countries must come forth with a plan for economic co-operation. . . . . Or will they develop a type of foreign trade bordering on exploitation which could cripple the development efforts of Africa? If this is what they are doing, then we do not hesitate to cry out, Beware of growing Arab imperialism.[4]

President Qadhafi has said that because of his country's oil wealth he could "buy the Africans," a comment which infuriated African politicians, journalists and scholars. When Uganda and Chad accepted Libyan money to sever relations with Israel, many African newspapers rebuked them. To accept such money, one paper said, was to sell oneself into slavery.

Africans repeatedly raise two questions for the Arabs:
- How much Arab oil money is being spent against the white regimes in the south — South Africa, Rhodesia and until recently, the Portuguese colonies? (Practically none, except in the case of Libyan aid to Angolan rebels.)
- How much oil money is going to the endemically drought-stricken countries such as Senegal, Mali, Mauritania, Chad, Niger and Upper Volta? (In fact, to September, 1975, less than one per cent of aid came from all the Arab countries together.)

When African countries began to realize that the Arab "oil weapon" damaged their economies as much as those of western countries, they appealed to the Arab states, through various African and Islamic conferences, for special concessions. They especially wanted lower prices and the establishment of refineries in Africa.

Instead, the Arabs proposed to set up an Arab bank with a capital of about 200 million dollars. The Africans, fearing a new hold over Black Africa through loans, asked that the money be given to an African development bank, but this was refused. The Arabs also told the Africans that for technical reasons and because lower priced oil might find its way to other markets, no concessionary oil prices could be permitted.

Once again, past grudges against the Arabs — such as the slave trade and imperialism — were raised. Ndolo Ayah, a leading Kenyan politician, recalled ". . . the previous experiences with the Arabs who commercialised in the slave trade, using Africans."[5]

---

[3]*Ibid.*
[4]*Liberian Age,* January 31, 1974.
[5]*Daily Nation,* June 19, 1974.

Epilogue

Joseph Nyerere, brother of the Tanzanian president, suggested that since the Nile rose in East Africa the countries at its source should charge Egypt and the Sudan for the use of the Nile waters. "Let us make a deal with the Arabs — a gallon of water for a gallon of oil, a barrel for a barrel."[6]

> African journalists were no less bitter than politicians. Refusal by Arab countries to sell oil to African states at a reduced price is a tacit example that Arabs, our former slave masters, are not prepared to abandon the rider-and-horse relationship. We have not forgotten that they used to drive us like herds of cattle and sell us as slaves.[7]

African disillusionment is so profound because hopes had been so high. "We thought the Arabs had changed," a Tanzanian scholar told me. "We hoped that they had reformed. But the slaver mentality obviously lasts longer than the slave mentality. We slave people were anxious to forget the terrible past but the past was not terrible for the Arabs so of course they remember. They still want slaves. All that has changed is their method of getting them."

---

[6] *Motherland*, New Delhi, June 17, 1974.
[7] *Zambia Daily Mail*, June 21, 1974.

Bibliography

Ali, Syed Ameer, *The Spirit of Islam* (London: Christophers, 1952).
Alpers, Edward A., *Ivory and Slaves in Central East Africa* (London: Heinemann, 1975).
Arberry, Arthur J., *The Koran Interpreted* (London: Oxford University Press, 1972).
Arnold, Sir Thomas and Guillaume, Alfred, eds., *The Legacy of Islam* (London: Oxford University Press, 1931).
Aubin, Eugene, *Le Maroc d'Aujourd'hui* (Paris, 1912).
Bahmat, Zubier Ibn, *Black Ivory and White or the Story of El Zubier Pasha, Slaver and Sultan, as told by himself* (London, 1910).
Baker, Samuel White, *The Albert N'Yanza* (London: 1866; republished London: Sidgwick & Jackson, 1962).
Barth, H., *Travels and Discoveries in North and Central Africa* (London: 1858; republished London: Frank Cass, 1964).
Batten, T. R., *Tropical Africa in World History* (London: Oxford University Press, 1939, 1973).
Bisch, Jorgen, *Behind the Veil of Arabia* (London: George Allen and Unwin, 1962).
Bovill, E. W., *The Golden Trade of the Moors* (London: Oxford University Press, 1958, 1970).
Burton, R. F., *Zanzibar, City, Island and Coast* (London, 1872).
Cabot Briggs, L., *Tribes of the Sahara* (London, 1960).
Colomb, R. N., *Slave Catching in the Indian Ocean* (London, 1873).
Coon, Carleton S., *Caravan: The Story of the Middle East* (New York: Holt, Rinehart & Winston, 1951).
Coupland, R., *The Exploitation of East Africa 1856 – 1890: The Slave Trade and the Scramble* (London: Faber and Faber, 1939, 1968).
idem, *East Africa and Its Invaders* (London: Oxford University Press, 1938).
Crabites, Pierre, *Gordon, the Sudan and Slavery* (London: George Routledge, 1933).
Darley, Henry, *Slaves and Ivory* (London: Witherby, 1926).
Denham, Dixon and Clapperton, Hugh, *Narrative of Travels and Discoveries in Northern and Central Africa* (London, 1826).
Derrick, Jonathan, *Africa's Slaves Today* (London: George Allen & Unwin, 1975).
Encyclopaedia of Islam. Edited by Professor R. Brunschwig, 1954 and 1962 editions. Gen. editors H.A.R. Gibb and J. H. Kramers. Leiden: E. J. Brill. The encyclopaedia has a 16 page entry on slavery in Islam.
El Tounssey, Sheikh Mohammad, ed., *Voyage au Ouaday* (Paris: Duprey et Jomar, 1851).

Farrant, Leda, *Tippu Tip and the East African Slave Trade* (London: Hamish Hamilton, 1975).
Farwell, Byron, *Prisoners of the Mahdi* (London: Longmans, 1967).
Fisher, Allan G. B. and Fisher, Humphrey J., *Slavery and Muslim Society in Africa* (London: Hurst, 1970).
Fuchs, Peter, *Land of the Veiled Men* (London: Faber, 1955).
Gautier, E. F., *Moeurs et Coutumes des Musulamans* (Paris, 1955).
Gooley, John K., *Baal, Christ and Mohammad* (London: John Murray, 1967).
Granqvist, Hilda, *Child Problems Among the Arabs* (Helsinki: Soderstom & Co., 1951).
Greeninge, Thomas, *Slavery* (London, 1958).
Hamady, Dr. Sonia, *Temperament and Character of the Arabs* (New York: Twayne Bros., 1960).
History of East Africa (London: Colonial Office, 1963).
Hourani, A.H. *Minorities in the Arab World* (London, 1947).
Humana, Charles, *The Keeper of the Bed: A Study of the Eunuch* (London: Arlington, 1973).
Ingrams, Doreen, *A Time in Arabia* (London: John Murray, 1970).
Ingrams, W. H., *Zanzibar, Its History and Its People* (London, 1931).
Keltie, James, *The Partition of Africa* (London, 1895).
Laffin, John, *The Arab Mind: A Need for Understanding* (London: Cassell, 1975).
Lewis, M., ed., *Islam in Tropical Africa* (London, 1966).
Livingstone, David, *Missionary Travels and Researches in East* Africa (New York, 1858).
Maugham, Robin, *The Slaves of Timbuktu* (London: Longmans, 1963).
Martelli, George, *Livingstone's River* (London: Chatto & Windus, 1970).
Moorehead, Alan, *The White Nile* (London: Hamish Hamilton, 1960).
Miner, Horace, *The Primitive City of Timbuktu* (New Jersey, 1953).
O'Callaghan, Sean, *The Slave Trade* (London: Anthony Blonde, 1961).
Oliver, Roland and Mathew, Gervase, eds., *History of East Africa,* Vol. 1 (London: Oxford University Press, 1963).
Owen, Roderic, *The Golden Bubble—Arabian Gulf Commentary* (London: Collins, 1957).
Richardson, James, *Travels in the Great Desert of Sahara* (London, 1840).
Schacht, J., *The Origins of Mohammadan Jurisprudence* (London: Oxford University Press, 1950).
Sim, Katherine, *Desert Traveller: The Life of Jean Louis Buckhardt* (London: Gollancz, 1969).
Slatin, Rudolf C., *Fire and Sword in the Sudan,* translated by F. R. Wingate (London: Edward Arnold, 1896).
Social Laws of the Koran (London: 1925).
Stanley, H. M., *Through the Dark Continent* (London: 1878).
Sullivan C. G. L., *Dhow Chasing in Zanzibar Waters and on the Eastern Coast of Africa. Narrative of Five Years' Experience in the Suppression of the Slave Trade* (London: 1873).
Swann, A. J. *Fighting the Slave Hunters in Central Africa* (London, 1890).
Thomas, Bertram, *The Arabs* (London: Thoenton Butterworth, 1938).
Trimingham, J. S., *Islam in the Sudan* (London: Frank Cass, 1965).
idem, *Islam in Ethiopia* (London: Oxford University Press, 1952).
Wellard, James, *The Great Sahara* (London: Hutchinson, 1964).
idem, *Desert Pilgrimage* (London: Hutchinson, 1970).
Young, Ian, *The Private Life of Islam* (London: Allen Lane, 1974).

891.4
DT
1317
L33
1982
L

Laffin, John.
 The Arabs as master slavers

OCT 26 '87	DATE DUE		

BETH HILLEL LIBRARY
WILMETTE, ILLINOIS

WITHDRAWN